DESIGN & DETAILS

DESIGN & DETAILS

CREATIVE IDEAS FOR STYLING YOUR HOME

Candie Frankel, Michael Litchfield, Candace Ord Manroe

MetroBooks

MetroBooks

An Imprint of Friedman/Fairfax Publishers

Copyright © 1998 by Michael Friedman Publishing Group, Inc.

Library of Congress Cataloging-in-Publication Data available upon request.

ISBN 1-56799-636-1

Editors: Sharyn Rosart, Hallie Einhorn,
Elizabeth Viscott Sullivan, and Francine Hornberger
Art Director: Jeff Batzli
Designers: Patrick McCarthy and Lynne Yeamans
Photography Editors: Jennifer Crowe McMichael,
Emilya Naymark, Colleen Branigan,
Samantha Larrance, and Wendy Missan
Layout: Terry Peterson and Charles Donahue
Production: Camille Lee and Susan Baumritter
Illustrator: Barbara Hennig

Color separations by Fine Arts Repro House Co., Ltd.
Printed in China by Leefung-Asco Printers Ltd.

For bulk purchases and special sales, please contact:
Friedman/Fairfax Publishers
Attention: Sales Department
15 West 26th Street
New York, NY 10010
212/685-6610   Fax 212/685-1307
Visit our website://www.metrobooks.com

Table of Contents

INTRODUCTION

When designing interiors, it is important that you think about many things at once. Many elements go into making a room—lighting, color, texture. To show off each to its advantage, all the separate parts must be considered as a whole. All the elements of a room must communicate with each other and not compete with one another for center stage. When all of the elements of a room come together in harmony, you can achieve an interior design treasure.

Visualizing how a room will come together is a task many do-it-yourself decorators find daunting, especially when the elements involved are not moveable items like furniture and paintings, but permanent features like tiled floors and recessed lighting. Making interior design choices is not unlike throwing a party. As host or hostess, you select guests from varying backgrounds who will enjoy one another's company, make the introductions that spark conversation, and make sure everyone is comfortable and happy. You want to create this same kind of harmony in your design.

Finding and orchestrating the right mix is also the interior designer's mission—and one that amateurs can readily pursue too. Good interiors are not simply about rooms looking good or feeding into someone's idea of style, they are about helping you live well. In everyday terms, this translates into obvious amenities—waterproof

Above: A SUCCESSFUL LIGHTING SCHEME ENCOMPASSES MANY ELEMENTS, AS DEMONSTRATED IN THIS KITCHEN. A WEALTH OF NATURAL LIGHT STREAMS IN THROUGH A LARGE WINDOW. RECESSED FIXTURES PROVIDE AN AMBIENT GLOW. TASK LIGHTING IS TAKEN CARE OF WITH DECORATIVE FIXTURES WHICH HANG FROM THE CEILING.

Opposite: A LIVING ROOM RICH IN TEXTURE IS GIVEN ITS RUSTIC FLAVOR THROUGH THE ROOM'S ARCHITECTURAL ELEMENTS: NAMELY, THE EXPOSED LOG WALLS AND CEILING BEAMS AND THE STONE, TWO-SIDED FIREPLACE.

—

floors in kitchens and bathrooms, ample lighting where you read, study, or chop vegetables—as well as features employed for pure pleasure. Good interiors use contrasting textures, architectural elements, and dramatic lighting to tease your sense of touch and space and turn rooms you use everyday into special places.

This anthology is based on the understanding that the bare bones of a room do matter. What you do with the walls and floors, where or whether you use recessed lighting, or what style and size mantel you install all affect the finished room as surely as the upholstery and window treatments you add later. How a room sizes up in the end depends on the groundwork laid in the beginning. Collected here are four topics anyone at the beginning of a design (or redesign) project would do well to consider: lighting, tiles, decorative paint treatments for walls, and architectural details.

Lighting is one of the most difficult aspects of design for people to work with, yet it is fundamental. The first section of this collection, Lighting Ideas, tackles lighting from an aesthetic as well as a practical viewpoint, proving that both are essential.

Natural light is free, and its effect on a room is very significant. Golden sunlight may be filtered by blinds, lace curtains, or a leafy outdoor tree that casts fluttering shadows within. Good interior design notes how and when daylight enters a room, how sunlight changes with the seasons, even what effect the changing weather has. A storm brewing outdoors can change the complexion of a room considerably.

At night, artificial lighting casts a different sort of spell. Soft pools of light from multiple fixtures around the room create a more romantic mood than the harsh glare of an overhead bulb. If overhead lighting is a must, a rheostat dimmer provides more control. Gently lit rooms are more healthy for us at night; they help our bodies wind down and prepare for sleep.

Choosing a lighting plan requires consideration of the fixtures themselves as well as the light they provide. Will the light source be hidden in the ceiling, or will a voluptuous lamp serve as both a decorative object and a light source? Is the light primarily for mood, or to help you get things done? In open floorplans, where dining and living areas flow together, recessed lighting and spotlights can emphasize parts of a room and throw less interesting corners into shadow. Task lighting beamed onto kitchen counters, desktops, and bathroom vanities is worth planning for when you remodel.

For all types of lighting, but particularly built-in lighting, preconstruction planning is essential. Think backwards from your vision of the finished room to provide adequate wiring for wall- and ceiling-mounted fixtures and outlets for freestanding lamps. A flowchart can help you organize the labor in a logical order. You don't want to paint a wall, only to have the electrician tear it open a few days later to install wiring for the sconces you ordered. Figure out what each project will entail, consider how the projects might impact each other, and then determine which project, or parts of projects, to tackle first. A kitchen remodeling, for example, might include installing wiring for above-counter task lighting, fitting in some architectural pieces you salvaged a few years back, tiling around them, and finally repainting the wall.

Tiles are a wonderful interior design tool, but next to other treatments such as paint and wallpaper, they can be expensive. But try not to let a high price tag deter you from exploring different types of tile that appeal to you. As you will see in the second part of this book, Designing with Tiles, most homes already have tiles in bathrooms,

and many homes use them to waterproof countertops, backsplashes, and floors in kitchens.

Tiles are not limited to use in kitchens and bathrooms, and they don't have to be the shiny ceramic variety. Walk through your home and consider which floor areas might be candidates for slate, stone, or polished marble tiles. If you love the look of tile, but your wood floors are too handsome to cover up, consider tiling just your foyer (the waterproof surface will be practical, especially if you live in a wet climate). Or you might enjoy a tiled fireplace surround. It doesn't have to be expensive; even broken shards can be assembled into a colorful mosaic, an idea

Above: This foyer demonstrates a successful integration of light, architecture, and tile. Natural lighting is provided by a skylight positioned directly over the circular railing. Clever square fixtures without excess ornamentation circle the perimeter of the space. Terra-cotta tiles give the massive, circular room a warm feel.

illustrated in several photographs in this section. Mosaic patterns provide a chance to be creative, and manufacturers make it easy by offering different sizes, shapes, and colors of tile designed to go together.

Tiles also can be used to convey mood and a sense of historical and geographical place. You can use baked terra-cotta or majolica tiles to carry out a Mediterranean decor, precision-cut marble tiles for a sophisticated classical, or irregular hand-built tiles that recall the Arts and Crafts period. In any room in your home, you can create drama with tile.

A less costly design option than tiles, using a textured wall paint treatment is a very effective design tool when your budget is limited.

A wall painted the right color can set a decorating scheme in motion. Use color to set any mood you desire, from light-hearted (try baby pink or yellow) to regal (deep violet or evergreen) to urbane (gray-green or taupe). Textured paint techniques are especially forgiving since additional glaze coats can modify the color in any direction you wish, from softer to more intense. Through them, your walls are never just one flat color but a composite of several color layers that vary according to the light and time of day. Also, if your walls are bumpy or uneven, a textured paint treatment easily hides imperfections. Paint-textured walls will make everything else you acquire—furniture, fabrics, lamps, rugs—look richer, fuller, and more vibrant.

Painting Textured Walls provides ideas for using common paint products to create wall surfaces that look decades, even centuries, old. Walls that appear cracked and patchy or worn and faded, will make an authentic backdrop to antique furnishings, yet are as easy to clean and care for.

Above: AN INTRICATELY DESIGNED PATTERN IN BLUES AND GREENS MAKES FOR AN EXCITING TILE BACKSPLASH IN THIS KITCHEN. THE THEME IS CONTINUED IN SMALLER SCALE ON A TILE BORDER THAT SURROUNDS THE KITCHEN AT COUNTER HEIGHT.

This section also shows how ordinary hallways and vestibules can be transformed into marble passageways. Faux stone, faux tortoiseshell, a sweeping panoramic mural, and trompe l'oeil designs are some of the other effects collected here. While many paint treatments are clearly the work of professional artists, some can be easily achieved by do-it-yourselfers; an appendix at the end of the book spells out the basics, including which paints and materials to use.

Lastly, Decorating with Architectural Details examines how glass, wood, stone, and metal artifacts can be worked into new construction as well as restorations to create the home of your dreams. It will also examine the value of salvage.

Some of the effects achieved using architectural details and salvage are dramatic: huge ornamental stonework that once adorned the façades of public buildings is now incorporated into the kitchens and living rooms of private homes. Old stained glass panels have been fitted into custom-made openings so they can be enjoyed again. From old churches and houses come wooden pediments, brackets, and moldings, used now to set off cozy alcoves or to offer visual, rather than struc-

tural, support. There's a place in the home for all manner of interesting, unconventional objects: old wrought-iron grilles, wavy-paneled shutters, stainless-steel elevator doors from an old medical building, even a vintage Coke machine turned into a dining room buffet table.

Objects salvaged from old buildings appear particularly compelling in new homes, imparting historical presence without forgoing modern amenities. This section shows how a simple yet striking mantel was made by anchoring an old hand-hewn beam to the wall above a contemporary fireplace made of used brick and hand-built by a mason who cavalierly threw away the rulebook. Arches, walkways, and patios pose inspiring possibilities for those patient enough to collect and build with salvaged brick and cobblestone. You may be compelled to acquire an item years before finding just the right use for it.

When all of these elements come together, you can create your dream room. This volume will help you define and distill your thoughts about the rooms you're decorating. Once your fantasy room takes shape, you'll be glad you thought about everything at once.

—Candie Frankel

PART ONE
LIGHTING IDEAS

INTRODUCTION

The exceeding brightness of this early sun

Makes me conceive how dark I have

become,

And re-illumines things that used to turn

To gold in broadest blue....

The Sun This March, *Wallace Stevens*

After the dazzle of day is gone,

Only the dark, dark night shows to my eyes

the stars;

After the clangor of organ majestic,

or chorus, or perfect band,

Silent, athwart my soul, moves the

symphony true.

After the Dazzle of Day, *Walt Whitman*

Natural light—be it the first glimmer of sunshine breaking on the horizon, the fiery parade of color marching across the western sky at day's end, or the mysterious illumination within the black velvet of night—is the stuff of poetry. Light does more than make the external world visible: In its infinite variations, it tugs at the emotions, creating moods that range from heady exuberance to quiet introspection, even melancholy.

It isn't just natural light that carries such power. Artificial light, working independently or in tandem with natural light, has the same potential for affecting mood and eliciting an emotional response. Consider the magical effect of the flickering light cast by a candle-lit chandelier, the eerie illumination produced by a red bulb, or the soft glow that emanates from a Japanese paper lantern.

Left: THE SOFT FLICKER OF CANDLELIGHT IS THE MOST INTIMATE LIGHTING CHOICE AND ONE THAT SHOULD NOT GO OVERLOOKED WHEN HIGH-INTENSITY ILLUMINATION IS NOT NECESSARY. FOR DINING, CONSIDER A CANDLELIT CHANDELIER SUPPORTED BY THE WARM LIGHT FROM A COLLECTION OF CANDLESTICKS ON THE TABLE AND SIDEBOARD.

Given light's power, it's not surprising that in recent years lighting has risen dramatically in importance as a consideration, and a tool, in interior design. Until recently, lighting was considered a merely utilitarian concern, like plumbing or wiring; today, however, it is recognized as a design element of some importance. Along with color, pattern, traffic flow, and other fundamental design concerns, lighting is now being planned in the conceptual phase of home design, instead of being an afterthought. An examination of a home's natural light sources—its windows, skylights, and French or atrium doors—is becoming as basic an undertaking as considering the home's palette and furniture style. The generic overhead room light, with its complement of tabletop lamps, though still viable, is no longer the automatic solution to lighting the home.

Instead, among savvy designers, architects, and do-it-yourself homeowners, lighting is being considered on a room-to-room, space-to-space basis, varying greatly from one place to the next depending upon the design goals. For example, in a room in which no single object or collection of *objets d'art* merits special attention, lighting may be diffused and moody, spreading a soft illumination throughout the space. In an area filled with beloved collectibles or art, the most effective lighting solution would be quite different, highlighting the desired objects with precise, direct light.

For a public space where a friendly feeling is desired, such as a family room, a traditional overhead fixture or chandelier might be the best artificial lighting choice, augmented by a vast wall of windows to bring in some welcome natural light. Even when the artificial lighting chosen is the standard overhead fixture, the room's mood can be changed by a device as simple and inexpensive as the reostat, or dimmer, which allows manipulation of the degree of light emitted.

In a highly architectural space, lighting, to realize its full potential, should underscore the architecture through a sophisticated blend of diverse light sources—a combination, perhaps, of up-, down-, and back-lights for evening,

Right: WHEN DESIGNING A HOME, THE PLACEMENT OF WINDOWS FOR TAKING ADVANTAGE OF NATURAL LIGHT AND VIEW SHOULD BE OF PRIME CONCERN. A SERPENTINE GLASS WALL IS INHERENT TO THE DESIGN STATEMENT OF THIS CONTEMPORARY HOME, DISSOLVING THE BOUNDARIES BETWEEN INDOORS AND OUTDOORS AND FLOODING THE SPACE WITH UNOBSCURED SUNSHINE.

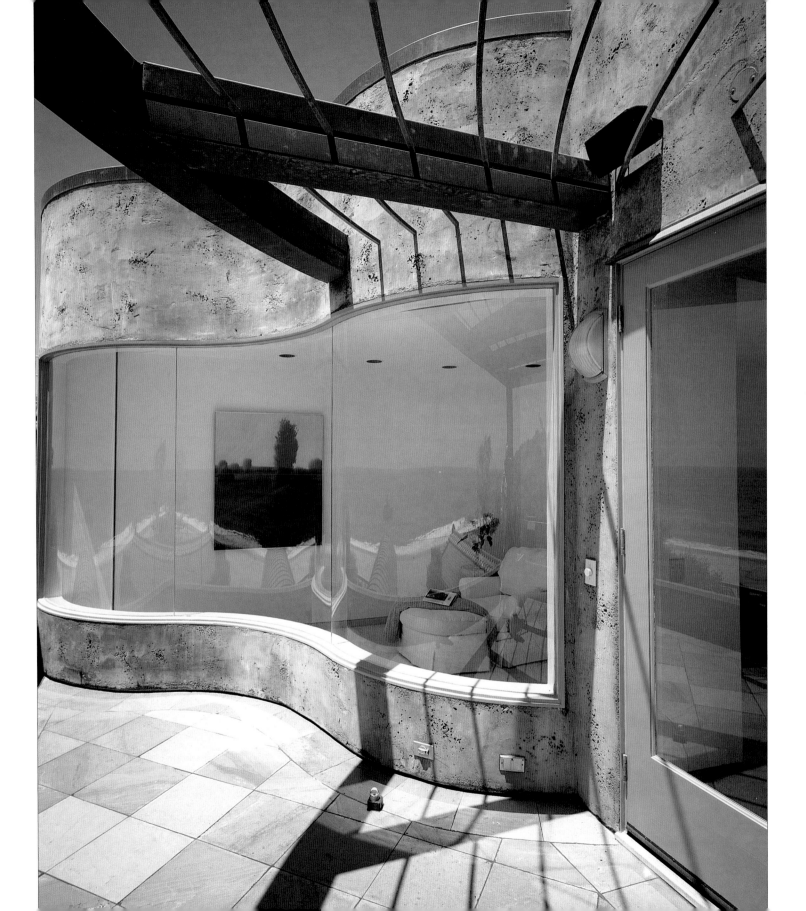

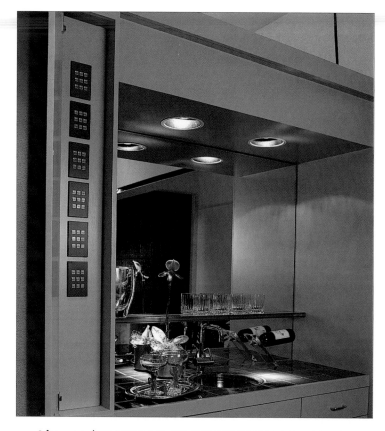

with carefully situated skylights, windows, and glass doors to maximize the architectural beauty during the day.

Lighting can be given unusual applications. For example, a light placed inside the marble steps of a staircase would create a beautiful, translucent glow. Even staple lighting solutions such as lamps can vary greatly in impact and mood when carefully chosen: Handmade parchment shades or the thin, filmy paper of Japanese lanterns impart a soft, ethereal glow much different from that of a more opaque shade, which diverts the direction of the light downward. Victorian beads and fringe also work to dapple lamplight, creating more interesting patterns of shadow and light than are possible with a uniform fixture or shade. For a home in which budget permits lighting to become art in its own right, laser lights—which require installation by licensed specialists—can bathe planes of color across a surface or highlight desired objects with deft precision.

In the kitchen and bath, where the function of lighting is especially important for accomplishing tasks, the idea of a single overhead light source is being regarded, more and more, as antiquated and ineffective. Instead, such choices as recessed fluorescent down-lights are appearing as a means of illuminating kitchen countertop work spaces, while back-lights at the tops of cabinets provide an aesthetically

Above: IN THIS WET BAR, RECESSED DOWN-LIGHTS SHINE THROUGH GLASS SHELVES, SIMPLY AND EFFECTIVELY ACCENTUATING THE ATTRIBUTES OF THE GLASSWARE.

pleasing way of showing off groupings of pottery, baskets, crystal, or other collectibles. In the bathroom, lighting can take a theatrical turn, becoming bold, bright, and abundant—perhaps outlining an entire mirrored wall—for aid in accomplishing such light-dependent tasks as shaving or applying make-up.

Lighting within the home can create romantic or conversational moods, select focal points, announce formality or casual living, and cater to the specific tasks required of a space. In the end, lighting can change how a space looks and how those within it feel. Why, then, the delay in lighting becoming a full-fledged design tool, indispensable in the decorating process?

Lighting has been underutilized in home design for several reasons. First, lighting requires more pre-planning than do some other decorating tools. It's easier to settle for overhead fixtures and lamps—and ignore the thought of changing the number and size of windows—than it is to explore more effective lighting treatments that might require special wiring on structural changes before the room design can be implemented.

Second, lighting doesn't offer immediate and continual gratification, as do some other decorating elements such as furniture or color. To appreciate the effects of lighting, it is necessary to wait until the appropriate time of day or night when the lighting is at its best: A strategically placed skylight offers its most dramatic effects only when the sun is shining; lush, moody artificial lighting works its magic only when the sun has set.

Another reason lighting has been dismissed as a serious design issue is because it is contingent upon other objects within the design to accomplish its goal. Exquisitely backlit architectural niches achieve nothing, unless objects worthy of such dramatic lighting are displayed within them. (A cache of clutter or loose pocket change and car keys, under such lighting, makes the whole lighting enterprise appear superfluous or even ridiculous.) Similarly, the fine stream of sunshine spilling down from a entry hall skylight accomplishes little, unless the entry's architecture, flooring, and furnishings merit such illumination.

Finally, lighting hasn't received the attention it deserves because many homeowners simply feel inadequate, having little knowledge about the technicalities involved in beautifully lighting a home. Rather than becoming knowledgeable or calling in a professional, many homeowners have opted to ignore the lighting challenge altogether, settling for existing natural light and the usual artificial light sources.

In the following chapters, examples of innovative lighting solutions—both natural and artificial—will illustrate the uses of lighting as a design tool, encouraging readers to explore some of the ideas in their own homes. As the following examples demonstrate, lighting can enhance or completely change the perception of a home and the pleasure it provides, without requiring the replacement of a single piece of furniture. For the serious home decorator, lighting in all of its dimensions, both natural and artificial, has too much potential power to go unexplored.

THE NATURALS

In home design, lighting is a constant interplay between natural and artificial light, an ever-changing dynamic that unfolds over the course of a day. To thoroughly address lighting in the home, the appearance of the home's spaces must be considered at all times of day, from early morning to midday to late night, with as much attention paid to the effects of sunlight as to the result of strategically placed artificial lights.

During the day, a room with only a few small windows can appear dark and stuffy and elicit feelings of claustrophobia, or a sense of being uncomfortably disconnected from the natural environment. A relatively easy and inexpensive way to lighten the mood—both of the home and of those within it—is the addition of skylights.

Especially welcome in an interior room that is altogether devoid of windows and any natural light (as is sometimes the case with small guest bathrooms), a skylight is the obvious answer for opening up the space and

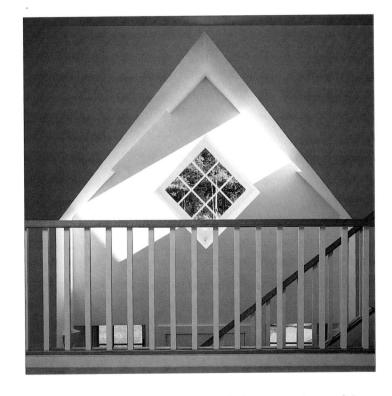

cheering it with the soft rays of the sun. Situated in a bedroom, above the bed, a skylight can have not only the daytime function of admitting golden light but the bonus of creating a romantic mood at night as well,

Above: MIMICKING THE ARCHITECTURE THAT SURROUNDS IT, A DIAMOND-SHAPED, SMALL-PANED WINDOW AT THE TOP OF A STAIRCASE WASHES THE WALL WITH JEWEL-LIKE NATURAL LIGHT DURING THE DAY, CALLING ATTENTION TO THE ARCHITECTURE. BY NIGHT, RECESSED LIGHTING SERVES THE SAME PURPOSE. **Left:** ANY PATTERN, COLOR, WINDOW TREATMENT, OR ART WOULD BE SUPERFLUOUS IN THIS BEDROOM, WHICH ACHIEVES ITS STELLAR GOOD LOOKS SOLELY THROUGH ITS UNIQUELY DESIGNED, ARCH-SHAPED COMBINATION OF GLASS DOORS WITH CONTEMPORARY INTERPRETATIONS OF THE FANLIGHT AND SIDELIGHTS.

allowing stargazing before sleep, and on a good night, a restful slumber in gentle puddles of moonlight.

As a design tool, a skylight serves one other function: Like artificial lighting, it can create a focal point within a space. At the top of a staircase, for example, the sunlight filtering down through a skylight onto the stairs below calls attention to the architecture, showcasing the grain of the wood and the lines of the staircase wall as though these were works of art.

When conceptualizing an interior design, many professionals begin with the windows—not the window treatments, but the windows themselves. For it is the light in a room, more than the ornamentation, that can most dramatically change the appearance of a space. Increasing the size of windows, when doing so does not interfere with the home's architectural lines and character, is often among the first objectives of design.

Even when standard-size rectangular windows aren't feasible, cutting a small round or more unusual octagonal window in the wall can totally alter the space's look and mood. Even a small amount of natural light can warm up a room significantly. For imparting a feeling of oneness with nature, an entire wall of windows is a wise design solution, with the boundaries between indoors and outdoors seeming to dissolve due to the transparency of the walls. In such a space, the design goal is not about creating a mood of intimacy, but rather one of expansiveness.

The most romantic light source, candlelight, is a transition between natural and artificial light. In designing the home, candlelight should be considered as a frequently used light source, not one that is merely occasionally introduced over a romantic dinner for two. The creative use of candles from candlelit chandeliers and sconces to permanent groupings of candlesticks on tabletops can create a wonderful ambience unlike that of either natural or artificial light. A similar feeling can be created with the flickering flames of oil lamps and lanterns.

Artificial lighting doesn't have to look artificial. Some of the most interesting interpretations emulate nature. Down-lights, whether spotlights or floodlights, can produce shafts of light akin to sunshine pouring through a window. Strands of tiny white lights encircling a room create the effect of a nighttime sky. Japanese paper lanterns emit a subtle, quiet glow akin to moonlight.

When planning lighting for the home, it's wise to keep in mind the origins of light, working closely with nature for the best results.

Above: A glass-block wall surmounted by skylights provides a creative solution to the problem of admitting natural light while still retaining privacy, and precludes the need for decorative window treatments. Filtered through the glass blocks, the light's interesting patterns are further accentuated by the open-grid stairway railing.

Above: BREATHTAKING RESULTS REWARD BUILDERS WHO GET TO KNOW THEIR SITE, THEN DESIGN THE HOME ACCORDINGLY, WITH WINDOWS PLACED TO CAPTURE THE MOST DRAMATIC PRESENTATIONS OF BOTH MORNING AND EVENING LIGHT. PROOF IS THIS SUNSET VISTA WITH ITS RICH COLORATION, ANTICIPATED IN THE PLANNING STAGES OF THE HOME, THAT COORDINATES WITH AND COMPLETES THE INTERIOR PALETTE. **Left:** AN UNDER-THE-EAVES LOFT BEDROOM ATTAINS A PRISTINE NATURAL BEAUTY WITH THE BENEFIT OF A SINGLE ROUND WINDOW, CUT IN THE CENTER OF THE WALL JUST ABOVE THE BED.

Above: An up-light creates a moody effect akin to natural, dappled light when shone upon a pedestal and sculpture. The light is positioned so that the illumination ascends the pedestal to reach the sculpture, creating an effect that is much more intriguing than that of a down-light shining directly upon the sculpture itself. **Right:** Floor-to-ceiling wood screens with a cane-like grid pattern dissipate the harshness of direct sunlight and create privacy when placed before the windows. They still permit sunlight into the room, however, throwing it into latticework shapes of light and shadow on the floor and furnishings.

Below: TO TRULY ADDRESS LIGHTING WHEN DESIGNING A SPACE, IT IS NECESSARY TO CONSIDER BOTH NATURAL AND ARTIFICIAL LIGHT IN TANDEM. THIS SPECTACULAR BATHROOM DESIGN SUCCEEDS IN USING LIGHT TO CREATE A DRAMATIC AMBIENCE: BY DAY, IT IS BATHED IN NATURAL LIGHT; BY NIGHT, RECESSED UP-LIGHTS AND DIRECTED DOWN-LIGHTS PROVIDE ILLUMINATION.

Above: WHEN ARCHITECTURE TAKES A VERTICAL EXPRESSION WITH AN EMPHASIS ON SOARING CEILINGS, A DARK, CAVERNOUS FEELING CAN RESULT. THIS ROOM CIRCUMVENTS THE PROBLEM WITH EXPANSES OF GLASS ON TWO WALLS THAT RISE ALL THE WAY TO THE CEILING, BATHING THE ROOM IN NATURAL LIGHT THAT CREATES AN AIRY, CHEERFUL ATMOSPHERE.

Below: WITH ITS LONGEST WALL DEVOID OF WINDOWS, THIS GALLEY-SHAPED BATHROOM MIGHT HAVE BEEN A STUDY IN DARKNESS. INSTEAD, THE ROOM IS WARMED BY SUNLIGHT STREAMING FROM SKYLIGHTS THAT SPAN THE ENTIRE LENGTH OF THE SPACE AND GLASS-BLOCK CORNER WALLS THAT ALLOW LIGHT INTO THE ROOM WITHOUT COMPROMISING THE NEED FOR PRIVACY. WITH THE NATURAL LIGHT AUGMENTED BY RECESSED DOWN-LIGHTS, THE BATHROOM THOROUGHLY ADDRESSES THE UTILITARIAN NEED FOR ADEQUATE LIGHTING TO PERFORM THE GROOMING TASKS ASSIGNED TO THE SPACE.

Above: NARROW SHAFTS OF LIGHT AND SHADOW CREATE A DAZZLING EFFECT IN THIS BATHROOM, IN WHICH A WIDE SKYLIGHT IS COVERED WITH CUSTOM-DESIGNED RATTAN BLINDS. THE STRIPED DESIGNS PRODUCED BY LIGHT FILTERING THROUGH THE BLINDS FALL ON VIRTUALLY EVERY SURFACE, INCLUDING THE WALLS, DOOR, AND TILE FLOOR.

Above left: As arteries between major living areas of the home, hallways are often sequestered from exterior walls, existing merely as dark and unappealing appendages. In this home, however, skylights make this passageway an aesthetic gem, dotting it with an interplay of light and shadow. **Above right:** The "eyes" of the home, windows are the feature to which we naturally gravitate. When conceived as a focal point of the design rather than as a staple element included by habit, a bank of windows can not only saturate a space with light but actually frame the outside view as though it was a work of art. **Right:** In a home in which the interior spaces ramble without access to exterior walls, a panel of skylights dominating the ceiling is an ideal solution for opening up the space and gracing it with welcome natural light.

Below: TINY DOWN-LIGHTS ILLUMINATE A DARK WOOD CEILING LIKE STARS IN A NIGHTTIME SKY. ARTIFICIAL LIGHTING'S EMULATION OF NATURE IS COMPLETED BY A GLOBE FIXTURE THAT HANGS LIKE A FULL MOON AMID THE SCATTERED PINPOINTS OF LIGHT.

Above: A PINT-SIZE KITCHEN WITHOUT WINDOWS RECEIVES SAVING GRACE FROM A SKYLIGHT GRID CENTRALLY PLACED IN THE ROOM. THE KITCHEN'S TRANSFORMATION FROM MERELY SALVAGEABLE TO HAVING ONE-OF-A-KIND STYLE IS COMPLETED BY A GLASS-BLOCK PANEL IN THE FLOOR THAT MIRRORS THE SKYLIGHT GRID OVERHEAD, REFLECTING ITS LIGHT.

Above: WHEN CREATIVITY IS GIVEN AS MUCH LICENSE IN THE DOMAIN OF LIGHTING AS IT IS IN OTHER DECORATING CONCERNS, THE EFFECT MAY BE AN UNEXPECTED AND WONDERFUL TURN OF FANCY, AS SEEN IN THIS BATHROOM. ITS WINDOWS ARE LARGELY DECORATIVE, BUT A MIRROR WITH STAINED-GLASS INSERTS THAT IS WRAPPED IN STRANDS OF TINY WHITE LIGHTS BRINGS BOTH ILLUMINATION AND A FESTIVE FLAIR TO THE SPACE.

Below: STRATEGIC PLACEMENT OF WINDOWS IS IMPORTANT FOR IMBUING A ROOM WITH THE APPROPRIATE AESTHETIC FEELING. THIS BATHROOM DERIVES ITS CHARACTER FROM THE BEAUTIFULLY PANED WINDOW THAT IS THE SPACE'S FOCAL POINT. POSITIONED AT THE TUB, THE WINDOW PERMITS CRISP MORNING LIGHT TO ENHANCE THE PLEASURE OF THE DAILY ROUTINE OF A SHOWER OR BATH.

Above left: PAPER LANTERNS POSSESS A SUBTLE, MOODY LUMINOSITY THAT IS AKIN TO MOONLIGHT ON WATER, IMPARTING A SERENE AND ROMANTIC FEELING THAT PRECLUDES THE NEED FOR MANY OTHER DECORATIVE ELEMENTS OR EVEN FURNISHINGS.

Above right: EVEN CONTEMPORARY LIGHT FIXTURES CAN CAPTURE THE ROMANCE OF CANDLELIGHT, AS SEEN BY THIS METAL AND GLASS PLATFORM CHANDELIER THAT IS HOST TO AN ARRAY OF VOTIVE CANDLES. THE SIMPLE BEAUTY OF THE VOTIVES IS REPEATED ON THE MANTELSHELF. **Left:** A SERIES OF IDENTICAL, DEEPLY RECESSED, SIMPLE RECTANGULAR WINDOWS POSITIONED NEAR THE CEILING ON TOWERING WALLS SCATTER SUNLIGHT ALONG THE CROWN OF THE ROOM—LIGHT THAT IS THEN REFLECTED ON THE DARK-STAINED CEILING FOR A MIRRORED EFFECT. THE SIMPLICITY AND FORM OF THE WINDOWS COMPLEMENT THE SPARE, LINEAR ARCHITECTURE OF THE SPACE.

Above: ANTIQUE LANTERNS NOT ONLY MAKE AN APPEALING COLLECTION, BUT WHEN LIT *EN MASSE*, AS IN THIS SHELVING NICHE, THEY PROVIDE AN INTRIGUING LIGHT SOURCE THAT DRAWS ATTENTION TO THE COLLECTION ITSELF. **Right:** LIKE CONSTELLATIONS, CIRCLES OF SPARKLING DOWN-LIGHTS IN THIS DINING ROOM BRING AN ETHEREAL NIGHTTIME MOOD TO THE DINING EXPERIENCE. THE ONLY OTHER LIGHT SOURCE NEEDED IS AN ELEGANT CANDELABRA.

SELECTIVE INTERESTS

Evenly dispersed light is flat—and dull. Without the shape and dimension created by areas of shadow or the contrast of bright and dim light, a room has little dynamic appeal. This holds true with both natural and artificial light. When morning sunlight filters through a window, it is the dappled effect that provides emotional appeal and visual interest. In an artificially lit room at night, it is the contrast of more and less illuminated surfaces that strikes a mood.

In planning lighting for the home, then, it's important to be selective—to determine which areas merit the most illumination and which are better falling into shadow. A simple, effective approach to lighting begins by taking inventory of the spaces and objects within a room: Decide which areas have the most interesting architecture and which objects would best serve as focal points.

Once this has been determined, add light accordingly by putting skylights over beautiful, serpentine plaster

Above: ARCHITECTURAL IN NATURE, THESE TALL CONTEMPORARY FLOOR LAMPS ARE GIVEN UNUSUAL APPLICATION AT THE WINDOWSILL, THEIR UP-LIGHTS ILLUMINATING THE TILED CEILING ABOVE INSTEAD OF THE FURNISHINGS BELOW. **Left:** SPOTLIGHTS ON TRACKS ABOVE THE WORK CENTERS OF THIS KITCHEN ADD A CONTEMPORARY FEEL TO THE ROOM DESIGN, WHICH IS A MIX OF RUSTIC AND CLEAN-LINED. BY THEIR PRECISE LOCATION, THE FIXTURES ALSO PERFORM THE UTILITARIAN FUNCTION OF ILLUMINATING THOSE SPECIFIC AREAS IN GREATEST NEED OF LIGHT.

walls; adding tiny pinpoints of artificial down-lights to call attention to worthy collectibles or art; placing recessed down-lights beneath cabinets or entertainment-center shelving to fall softly on the objects below; or situating back-lights within shelving to mysteriously highlight displays of glassware, crystal, or minerals.

Canister up-lights create exquisite effects on otherwise bare walls, on *objets d'art*, or even on plants, throwing shadows from the ficus tree against the wall in a mottled pattern similar to the lacy quality of shadows created by sunlight itself. Shining through a glass table or pedestal, up-lights add a diffused, moody quality of romance and mystery to a room. Track lighting with floodlights creates a gallery effect, leaving little mistake about the importance of the objects benefiting from this high-intensity illumination. Fluorescent lights inset under a cabinet to illuminate a work space or the objects below achieve yet a different look, creating a diversity that adds to the overall visual interest of the space.

The most successful lighting solutions are those most closely tailored to fit the other elements in the home's design. In a dining room, for instance, it may be understood that the area deserving attention as the key light source is the space above the dining table. If the dimensions and shape of the dining table are known before the lighting is installed, lighting can be adapted to blend harmoniously with the furniture. A large, round table, for example, might be lit by a circle of recessed down-lights of a similar circumference, placed directly above the space designated for the table. If other furnishings in the room are identified, secondary light sources can be planned to complement those objects—with up-lights to bring a soft, patterned glow to plants and small spotlights to accentuate works of art. For the most dynamic design, try lighting the home with a number of different light sources of varying intensities and qualities.

Lighting the home is a matter of prioritizing, determining which areas should be highlighted and which can recede, or identifying a primary light source augmented by secondary sources. Then it's all creativity, using your imagination to shed the most effective or evocative light on the scene.

Right: ARCHITECTURE AND LIGHTING GO HAND IN HAND, ONE REINFORCING THE OTHER'S EFFECTS. IN THIS UPPER-STORY SPACE, THE ABSTRACT ARCHITECTURAL PLANES ARE OUTLINED BY INDIRECT LIGHTING INSET INTO THE NEGATIVE SPACES OF THE CONFIGURATIONS.

Left: SCONCES SHINE LIGHT UP ABOVE THIS ROOM'S PANELED WALLS UPON ITS RICHLY LACQUERED MOLDINGS, MAKING THEM SHIMMER LIKE DARK POOLS OF WATER IN THE SOFT ILLUMINATION. INDIVIDUAL LAMPS ARE USED WHEN MORE ILLUMINATION IS REQUIRED.

Right: IN A TRADITIONAL HOME THAT BOASTS AN IMPORTANT ART COLLECTION, THE ELEGANCE OF CRYSTAL SCONCES IS NOT ENOUGH. EACH PAINTING MERITS A LIGHT OF ITS OWN, IN ORDER TO RECEIVE FULL RECOGNITION AMID THE DISPLAY OF OPULENCE.

Above left: UP-LIGHTS INSET BEHIND CROWN MOLDING IN A GAP BETWEEN THE CEILING AND WALLS PROVIDE A GENTLE, UNUSUAL LIGHT FOR THIS DINING ROOM, AN ALTERNATIVE OR ADDITIONAL LIGHT SOURCE TO THE CONTEMPORARY CHANDELIER ABOVE THE TABLE. **Above right:** BEFORE PLANNING HOW TO LIGHT A ROOM, IT IS NECESSARY TO DETERMINE THE FOCAL POINT OF THE SPACE. IN THIS DINING ROOM, THE TABLE AND ADJACENT ART ARE HIGHLIGHTED BY DIRECTIONAL DOWN-LIGHTS MOUNTED ON A CEILING PLATFORM. PEEKING AROUND THE PERIMETER OF THE PLATFORM IS A SOFTER, DIFFUSED LIGHT THAT GIVES THE ENTIRE SPACE A MUTED GLOW.

Above: The more serious the home chef, the more important lighting becomes in the kitchen. Here, windows and skylights let in daylight, while a succession of floodlights illuminates key work spaces, and compatible track lighting provides a more uniform light on storage spaces.

Right: Recessed spotlights can be precisely directional, pinpointing illumination down upon key areas. In this serene bedroom, spots shine directly on three works of art.

Above left: ADVANCE PLANNING IS ESSENTIAL IN ACHIEVING THIS SUBTLE YET HIGHLY DRAMATIC BACKLIGHTING ON GLASS SHELVES OF *OBJETS D'ART*. NOTE THE INTEREST CREATED BY THE CONTRAST IN TONE BETWEEN THE GOLDEN TUBE LIGHT AND THE SOFTER BLUE-GREEN BACK-LIGHTS. **Above right:** A SMALL, RECESSED DOWN-LIGHT ILLUMINATES THIS POWDER ROOM FROM ABOVE, WHILE A PAIR OF TUBE LIGHTS FLANKING THE MIRROR EFFECTIVELY PROVIDE THE BRIGHT CLARITY NECESSARY TO MAKE THE ROOM FUNCTIONAL. **Right:** LAMPLIGHT AND A DOUBLE-GLOBE SCONCE DRAW THE EYE TO THIS CHARMING BEDSIDE STILL LIFE OF PHOTOGRAPHS, CHINA, AND FLOWERS.

Above: A COMMON MISTAKE IN LIGHTING A ROOM IS TO ASSUME THAT DOWN-LIGHTS MUST BE CENTRALLY PLACED TO SHED LIGHT ACROSS THE ENTIRE SPACE. A MORE INTERESTING SOLUTION IS TO POSITION THEM SELECTIVELY, AS SEEN HERE ABOVE THE TUB IN THIS RUSTIC COUNTRY-STYLE BATHROOM. **Right:** THESE CUSTOM-DESIGNED NEOCLASSICAL ARMOIRES WITH OPEN LATTICEWORK PEDIMENTS CREATE A STRONG DESIGN STATEMENT WHEN LIT FROM WITHIN, MAKING THE PEDIMENTS INTO GLOWING CROWNS OF LINEAR PATTERN. RECESSED OVERHEAD LIGHTS SHINING INTO AND AROUND THE ARMOIRES ADD A WARM WHISPER OF ILLUMINATION TO THE SPACE.

AUGUST SANDER: CITIZENS OF THE TWENTIETH CENTURY · GUNTHER SANDER, EDITOR

Chandeliers and Lamps

Before recessed lighting, track lights, canister lights, and laser lighting, chandeliers and lamps served the primary lighting needs in the home. These traditional lighting solutions remain strong contenders in home design, but in the *best* designs, they are no longer considered the obvious or only answer. Nevertheless, when used in concert with other lighting solutions, chandeliers and lamps can be vital, attractive components in the well-designed room.

While chandeliers and lamps make design statements through the light they emit, they differ from other artificial lighting sources by also making design statements that have nothing to do with light itself but with the style—the appearance—of the lighting vessel. Therein lies their strength, their continued popularity, and their ensured longevity in interior design. Because they are decorative as well as functional, chandeliers and lamps can add to the articulation of a room's style in a way no other form of artificial light can.

The good news in decorating is that manufacturers have finally begun to address lamps and chandeliers as design issues, approaching their form and style with the same creativity that is brought to other furnishing design. The basic

Above: For illuminating everyday lifestyle activities such as plopping down in an easy chair or on a sofa with a good book, table lamps provide a time-tested solution. Here, a pair of matched contemporary lamps serves this practical function, while also visually uniting the room. Left: Amid a display of photography, a hand-painted lampshade with delicate silk tassel trim adds elegance, color, and artistic design, while casting intriguing patterns of light and shadow on the photo collection itself.

brass or ginger-jar lamp and the typical crystal chandelier, while remaining classics, have been augmented with a wealth of other lighting designs that encompass all styles, tastes, and colors.

A contemporary room that is essentially architectural in character can now be complemented by Italian-designed metal lamps that are architecture in their own right. A room designed in the popular lodge look—a rustic camp style—can now have its style underscored by a magnificent twig chandelier.

For the collector's home, almost any small antique, from a Staffordshire figurine to an old Chinese wedding basket to a brass horn, can be adapted into a lamp. For the home in which texture is the primary source of design interest, lamps and chandeliers are available in such diverse materials as iron, rattan, wood, bone, glass, and clay. Newly manufactured lamps and chandeliers include period reproductions of every historic type, as well as whimsical creations that are one-of-a-kind.

While a chandelier may not be the best solution for every room in the home, it's hard to imagine a home in which at least one overhead fixture is not appropriate. And it is a stretch to conceive of a home (except, perhaps, one with the most minimalistic design) in which lamplight isn't a practical, as well as aesthetic, strong suit. When choosing the favorite standbys of chandeliers and lamps, consider these lighting solutions as additions to a larger lighting scheme that involves other light sources. Take into account the effect of the light—not all chandeliers or lamps create the same type of lighting—and ensure that the style of the chandeliers and lamps captures the design theme of the space.

Above: TWO CONTEMPORARY CHANDELIERS BRING SPRIGHTLY COLOR TO THE ROOM WITH THEIR STACKED PRIMARY-COLORED DISKS. INSTEAD OF DIRECTING LIGHT DOWNWARD, AS DO MOST CEILING FIXTURES, THESE DIFFUSE LIGHT SIDE-WAYS, CREATING A SOFTER LIGHT SOURCE.

Above: PROOF THAT '50S FURNITURE IS UNDERGOING A REVIVAL, THIS ROOM'S UP-TO-THE-MINUTE RETRO LOOK IS DRAMATIZED BY A MULTI-GLOBED FLOOR LAMP THAT ADDS ESSENTIAL HEIGHT, AS WELL AS LIGHT, TO THE SPACE'S COLLECTION OF LOW-SLUNG FURNISHINGS. VENETIAN BLINDS CREATE THEIR OWN MOODY EFFECT BY DAY WHILE ENHANCING THE '50S THEME.

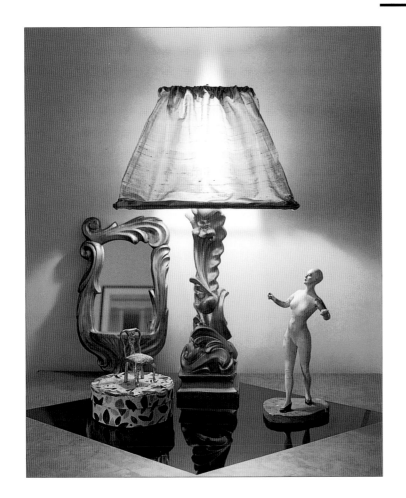

Above left: THIS SMALL TABLE LAMP IS AN *OBJET D'ART* IN ITS OWN RIGHT; WHEN GROUPED WITH OTHER SMALLER ACCESSORIES, IT IS THE FOCAL POINT OF A TABLETOP STILL LIFE, LENDING THE NECESSARY SCALE AND GLOW THAT BALANCE THE ARTFUL COMPOSITION. **Above right:** ONCE A SADLY NEGLECTED AREA OF HOME FURNISHINGS IN TERMS OF INNOVATIVE DESIGN AND MATERIALS, LAMPS TODAY HAVE COME INTO THEIR OWN AS ARENAS OF CREATIVITY, AS PROVEN BY THIS CONTEMPORARY LAMP WITH ITS ARTFUL, TRANSLUCENT PAPER SHADE FORMED IN AN IRREGULAR, TWISTED SHAPE.

Left: HANDCRAFTED LAMPSHADES REPRESENT CLASSIC TURN-OF-THE-CENTURY ARTS AND CRAFTS STYLE IN LIGHTING. THESE CRAFTSMAN LAMPS ARE AUTHENTIC COMPLEMENTS TO A ROOM DECORATED WITH MISSION FURNISHINGS CREATED DURING THE SAME DESIGN MOVEMENT.

Below: NEOCLASSICAL CANDLESTICK LAMPS COMPLEMENT THE NEUTRAL ELEGANCE OF THIS SILVERY BATHROOM, WHILE SERVING THE UTILITARIAN FUNCTION OF ILLUMINATING THE MORNING TOILETTE. LAMPS, COMMONLY FOUND IN BEDROOMS AND LIVING AREAS, ARE SOMEWHAT UNEXPECTED IN THE BATHROOM, THEREBY ADDING GREATER VISUAL INTEREST TO THE SPACE.

Above: VICTORIAN FRINGE CREATES A LIGHTING EFFECT DIFFERENT FROM THAT OF AN UNTRIMMED SHADE, CHANGING THE INTENSITY OF THE LIGHT LIKE A SCREEN. HERE, IT CASTS A SOFT GLOW OVER A COLLECTION OF OLD PHOTOGRAPHS.

Below: A CONTEMPORARY DESK LAMP WITH A COLORED-GLASS GLOBE MAKES A SLEEK DESIGN STATEMENT IN A HOME OFFICE SPACE DOMINATED BY CONTEMPORARY WALL ART.

Above: THE UNIQUE STYLING OF THIS BEDROOM WITH ITS ECLECTIC COLLECTIBLES WOULD BE ILL SERVED BY A BLAND LAMP. THE RIGHT SOLUTION IS ONE THAT ENHANCES THE ROOM'S INDIVIDUALITY, LIKE THIS CERAMIC BEDSIDE LAMP WITH ITS TURBANED-HEAD BASE AND TEXTURED PAPER SHADE.

Above: An Art Nouveau bronze figurine rising up from a newel post serves as an arresting lamp to shed light on the ascent up the stairs. **Left:** Among the main draws of lamps are the unlimited possibilities they offer for creative expression. Almost any favorite collectible can be adapted and wired to function as a lamp, as illustrated by this dressmaker's dummy turned chairside lamp.

Above left: A LASSOING COWBOY BECOMES A CONVERSATIONAL ITEM WHEN TRANSFORMED INTO THE BASE OF A TABLE LAMP IN A SOUTHWESTERN-STYLE ROOM. **Above right:** PAPER SCONCES PATTERNED WITH INKY DINOSAURS CAST A SURREAL GLOW ON THE WALL. THE BLACK PICTORIAL DESIGN STANDS IN STRIKING CONTRAST TO THE GOLDEN BACKGROUND. **Right:** WITH ITS ELONGATED IRON BASE, THIS FLOOR LAMP REPRESENTS THE BEST OF POPULAR OLD WEST DESIGN AS A MELDING OF RUSTIC TEXTURE AND CLASSIC NATIVE AMERICAN MOTIFS.

Below: AS MUCH A CONTEMPORARY SCULPTURE AS A LIGHTING FIXTURE, THIS TREE LAMP FEATURES SINEWY IRON BRANCHES BEARING GOLDEN CYLINDERS OF LIGHT.

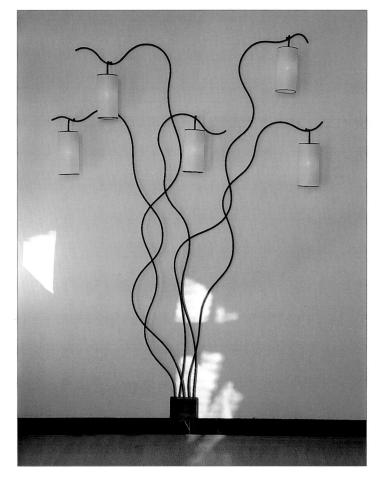

Above: A CONTEMPORARY CLASSIC, THIS ARCHITECTURAL LAMP COMPLEMENTS THE ROOM'S MODERN DESIGN AND ARCHITECTURE WHILE ALSO SERVING THE PRACTICAL FUNCTION OF PROVIDING A GOOD READING LIGHT.

Left: IN A BOLD, CONTEMPORARY ROOM IN WHICH EACH FURNISHING HAS A DISTINCTIVE, SCULPTURAL FORM, PAPER LANTERNS PLAY AN INTEGRAL ROLE IN ARTICULATING THE DESIGN THEME WITH THEIR GEOMETRIC SHAPES AND STARK SIMPLICITY.

Above left: AN ANTIQUE ART-GLASS CHANDELIER OF SUBSTANTIAL SCALE LENDS PERIOD CHARM TO A STATELY ROOM, WHILE ALSO SERVING TO DEFINE THE ROOM'S FOCAL POINT—THE EXQUISITE INLAID MARBLE TABLE. **Above right:** A PAIR OF CANDLESTICK LAMPS BRINGS UNDERSTATED ELEGANCE TO A DECORATIVE CONSOLE TABLE CAPPED WITH AN OPULENTLY CARVED MIRROR IN WHICH CAN BE SEEN THE REFLECTION OF A GLOWING CHANDELIER. **Right:** DARK METAL STAR SCONCES FORCE LIGHT BEHIND AND AROUND THEIR DISTINCTIVE SHAPE, CREATING A CHARMING HALO EFFECT. THE ROOM ALSO UTILIZES DOWN-LIGHTS FOR FOCUSING UPON THE ART AND THE ARCHITECTURAL MIRROR.

Left: As with other aspects of decorating, attention to detail in lighting rewards the effort with great results. Here, antique glass globes with delicate, lacy patterns imbue a chandelier with a rich, erstwhile character. Below: As lighting becomes an increasingly popular area for creativity in design, some unique fixtures are available. Fashioned from kitchen equipment, beads, and other unusual elements, this witty and functional chandelier provides the room with both light and a sense of fun.

Left: The sophisticated lighting plan in this dining room includes a recessed down-light in the niche and spots that focus light down from the ceiling, but the outstanding feature is the custom-made Mexican chandelier. Its armature has been softened by a grapevine wrapping, while its unique lamps are made of stainless-steel mesh molded into flame-like forms. The result is a wonderful interplay of light and shadow that both provides illumination and creates a dramatic yet intimate mood.

Above: FOR SOME ROOMS, THE INCOMPARABLE ELEGANCE OF A TRADITIONAL CHANDELIER

REMAINS THE PERFECT CHOICE. IN THIS GRAND CIRCULAR FOYER SPANNING TWO

STORIES, THE CHANDELIER IS THE *PIÈCE DE RÉSISTANCE*. **Right:** IN THIS OPULENT LIVING

ROOM, A FINE CRYSTAL CHANDELIER MAKES A STATEMENT OF REFINED GRACE.

Above: LIKE THE CABIN OF A HOT-AIR BALLOON, THE PETITE LIGHTING PORTION OF THIS OVERHEAD FIXTURE IS SUSPENDED BY SHEER WHIMSY, ENHANCING THE ROOM'S APPEALING COTTAGE CHARM. **Right:** A FRINGED TIFFANY-STYLE GLASS VICTORIAN CHANDELIER BRINGS TURN-OF-THE-CENTURY WARMTH TO A HEAVILY PANELED DINING AREA THAT FEATURES A LACE-DRAPED TABLE.

Above: THE LIGHTING TREATMENT FOR THIS ELONGATED ISLAND BAR IS A VARIATION ON OVERHEAD CHANDELIERS: INSTEAD OF A SINGLE CHANDELIER, THREE SMALL CONTEMPORARY LIGHTS DANGLE CLOSE TO THE WORK SPACE FROM LONG RIBBONS OF CABLE.

Above: Despite its electrified-candle form, there is nothing traditional about this dining room chandelier, with its rustic, free-form twig design that is an ideal companion to the table base below.

Above: RATHER THAN OVERWHELMING WITH OPULENCE, THIS GRACEFUL ANTIQUE CHANDELIER CONVEYS A SPIRIT OF RESTRAINED FINERY WITH ITS DELICATE FORM, SCALE, AND MATERIALS. **Left:** THE KEY TO THE EFFECTIVENESS OF THIS TURN-OF-THE-CENTURY CRAFTSMAN CHANDELIER LIES IN ITS UNEXPECTED PLACEMENT JUST INCHES ABOVE THE DINING TABLE—A CHOICE THAT REVEALS THE REWARDS OF PLANNING AND A WILLINGNESS TO BEND RULES.

Above: SUSPENDED FROM IRON CHAINS AND OUTFITTED WITH APPROPRIATE LIGHTING HARD-
WARE, AN OLD WAGON WHEEL MAKES A UNIQUELY APT CHANDELIER FOR A ROOM DECORATED IN AN
AMERICAN SOUTHWEST STYLE. **Right:** AN ENORMOUSLY HIGH CEILING REQUIRES A LONG CABLE
TO BRING A CHANDELIER DOWN TO HUMAN LEVEL, WHERE THE CONTEMPORARY FIXTURE
CAN SHED LIGHT ON A DINING TABLE.

PART TWO

DESIGNING WITH TILES

INTRODUCTION

Probability says that tiles appear somewhere in your home. Waterproof and easy to clean, standard glazed ceramic tiles are commonplace in bathrooms and kitchens. With function figuring so prominently in their installation, it's easy to overlook the vibrant, extensive decorating potential of even the most ordinary household tiles. Tiles can add color, pattern, and texture to walls, floors, entryways, fireplaces, staircases, door frames, and a host of other architectural elements. They can be used indoors and out, in both obvious and not-so-obvious places. Special corner edgings,

hand-painted or printed motifs, and an array of materials, sizes, and surface finishes make the tile options for any home broad indeed.

In use since antiquity, tiles have an interesting and impressive history. They have lined the inner chambers of pyramids and have long been associated with bathing. In the Islamic world, individual tiles were painted with repetitive floral and botanical motifs that created continuous swirling patterns when the tiles were arranged side by side on a wall or floor. In medieval England, radiating circular patterns were created on the floors of churches and abbeys by butting together tiles of different colors and interlocking geometric shapes. Different regions developed their own signature styles for painted tiles, resulting, for example, in the blue-and-white delft tiles of Holland and

Opposite: IN ORDER TO IMPART A TRADITIONAL FLAVOR, THIS CONTEMPORARY OPEN-PLAN KITCHEN RELIES ON A CLASSIC CHECKERBOARD TILE BACKSPLASH, OLD-FASHIONED BRASS HINGES AND DRAWER PULLS, AND GLAZED CABINET DOORS. EVEN THOUGH THE KITCHEN IS EQUIPPED WITH EVERY MODERN CONVENIENCE, THE OVERALL DECOR REMAINS NOSTALGIC, RECALLING TILED KITCHENS OF THE EARLY TWENTIETH CENTURY. AGAINST THE PLAIN WHITE CABINETRY AND WALLS, THE NAVY AND GRAY BACKSPLASH TILES POP OUT WITH GEOMETRIC PRECISION. HIGHER UP ON THE WALL, A TAUPE SHADE REPLACES THE GRAY IN A COORDINATING TILED FRIEZE. **Above:** WHEN A BATHROOM REMODELING IS IN THE PLANNING STAGE, ARRANGING LOOSE TILES SIDE BY SIDE ON A FLAT SURFACE CAN MAKE DIFFERENT DESIGN CONFIGURATIONS EASIER TO VISUALIZE. HERE, THE PLAIN SQUARE TILES UNDER CONSIDERATION FOR A SHOWER STALL ARE INTERSPERSED WITH A SELECTION OF SCULPTED BORDER TILES. THE INTRODUCTION OF JUST A SINGLE BORDER CAN HELP BREAK UP AN ORDINARY FOURSQUARE GRID AND MAKE A BATHROOM MORE INTERESTING WITHOUT SUBSTANTIALLY INCREASING THE BUDGETED COST.

the bright majolica tiles of Portugal, Spain, Italy, and Mexico.

While tiles have traditionally been admired for their handcrafted beauty and magnificent designs, today they are also sought for their engineered precision and striking modernity. The newest tiles to enter home decor are made not of clay or porcelain but of natural stone that is mined from the earth's quarries. White, russet, green, and black marble, purplish shades of slate, creamy gray limestone, and peppery granite are among nature's exquisite offerings. Computers direct the machinery that cuts the stones to precise dimensions and thicknesses, producing beautiful, uniformly sized tiles that can be polished to a mirror finish. Laid down in a crisp black-and-white checkerboard across a foyer floor or stretched across a kitchen backsplash, tiles such as these impart a sense of luxury and glamour to ordinary household routines.

Even though most people have an idea of the types of tile they like and don't like, actually choosing tiles from the vast selection available can be overwhelming. Clipping pictures of tiles from decorating magazines and studying books such as this can help you zero in on a special style or composition more readily than a tile retailer's sample books, which don't always show the most innovative installations but instead concentrate on standard looks that will appeal to the broadest range of people. If you want to do something special with colors, or think you might like to try mosaic tile on your bathroom floor, you should discuss your ideas directly with a tile contractor, preferably one with a reputation for innovative, custom work. (Unless you have previous experience, tile installation by a professional is the route to go for a quality job.) If you are embarking on a major kitchen or bath remodeling, you will be working

Above: DISTINCTIVE ARCHITECTURAL FEATURES, SUCH AS THIS ARCHED FIREPLACE MANTEL, GAIN PROMINENCE WHEN ACCENT TILES FOLLOW THE SAME CONTOURS. HERE, EDGING TILES WERE SELECTED FOR THEIR PROTRUDING LIP, WHICH BUTTS UP AGAINST THE MANTEL'S CURVED, WHITE WOODWORK. WITH THE ADDITION OF A SPECIALLY MOLDED CORNER TILE, THE LIP GRACEFULLY DESCENDS INTO A DELICATE CURLICUE.

with a general contractor and perhaps a designer, both of whom can help you develop and incorporate your design ideas into the overall scheme.

Color and overall look are the exciting aspects of designing with tiles, but aesthetics are not the only consideration. Equally important are a tile's maintenance requirements and its appropriateness for the intended use. Ceramic tiles that have been designed for floors, for example, are thicker and more durable than those manufactured for walls, which would crack under normal foot traffic. Unglazed terra-cotta tiles can give a beautiful, earthy tone to a dining room, but they are not suitable for bathroom floors, which need to be waterproof. By reading various tile manufacturers' literature and examining tile samples in the showroom, you will gain a feel for the quality, thickness, density, and texture of the different varieties of tile. Some tile showrooms will even let you borrow a sample tile for a day or two so that you can examine it under the lighting conditions in your own home.

Discovering new ways to incorporate tiles into the decor of living areas, kitchens, and bathrooms is a fascination that will never cease. Choosing tiles may be a challenge, but as the photographs on the following pages show, living with them is easy. Simultaneously beautiful and utilitarian, tiles are great mood creators, adorning the surfaces of ordinary homes with the marble favored by kings, the terra-cotta clay of peasants, and the provincial painted designs of tile artisans. Used throughout history, tiles are familiar objects that possess decorative powers far exceeding their humble origins, and perhaps therein lies the secret of their unending allure.

Above: Multiple colors and detailed patterns can be the result of intricate hand-set tiles—or trompe l'oeil tiles like these. The eight-pointed blue star designs look as though they were assembled from individual triangles and squares, but each one was actually created by glaze patterns on a single, larger square tile. More diamond and triangle patterns create the same illusion on coordinating rectangular border tiles. White grout lines distinguish the real tiles from the glazed-on patterns.

TILES UNDERFOOT

The one place where tiles can be found in all different types of rooms is on the floor. Of the many uses to which tiles can be put, paving a floor is their most basic job. From first-century Roman courts to twentieth-century department stores, tiles have always appeared in public spaces, making floors easier to walk on and providing a decorative backdrop for people's public lives. In the home, floor tiles are a more private matter, given to both fantasy and practicality. They can simulate the marble halls of a palace or the sun-baked piazza of a Mexican village. There is great pleasure in being vicariously transported to these and other places one loves by simply walking around one's own home and looking down on a tiled floor.

The beauty of a tile floor goes hand in hand with good housekeeping. Like the good-grooming dress code that advises people to buy the best quality shoes they can afford so that the heels will not wear down, the first principle of interior design is to invest in, not skimp on, a good-looking floor. Glazed ceramic, cut stone, terra-cotta, and mosaic are among the high-quality, long-wearing tiles that can bring the integrity and beauty of natural materials to a room for years on end, yet require only minimal care. When a beautiful tile floor is underfoot, even a sparsely furnished room can look rich and elegantly appointed instead of shabby or underdressed.

The photographs that follow show a variety of tile floors in settings throughout the home. They offer a first look at different types of tiling materials, revealing their surface textures and colors, as well as designs, grids, and patterns that work well on floors.

Opposite: Instead of an area rug, shiny glazed turquoise tiles decorate the floor of a dining porch, safely dispensing with any floppy rug corners or long fringe that could trip up traffic in this busy family gathering space. Next to the warm-hued, matte-finish quarry tiles that cover the rest of the floor, the blue tiles take on an exceptionally glassy sheen and, under certain lighting conditions, look as though they are illuminated from within. Above: Affordable souvenirs of a vacation, tiles purchased in small quantities can be a novel addition to home decor. Here, a collection of hand-painted tiles bought at a market in Mexico finds a home along three risers leading to a clay-tiled terrace. Used in this way, the tiles can be enjoyed every day, serving as a reminder of the trip while bestowing a permanent gift of handcrafted beauty on the home.

Above: LAID ON THE DIAGONAL, SQUARE CERAMIC TILES IN A CLASSIC CHECKERBOARD PATTERN APPEAR AS DIAMONDS, BREAKING UP THE ROOM'S BOXY ARCHITECTURE. UNLIKE BLACK AND WHITE TILES, WHICH CREATE A HIGH CONTRAST, THE APRICOT AND BLUE-GRAY COLORS USED HERE ARE MUCH CLOSER IN TONE, PRODUCING A SOFTER, LESS DRAMATIC EFFECT. THE SAME MARBLE-LOOK FLOOR TILES EXTEND AROUND THE FIREPLACE, DRESSING UP THE PLAIN OPENING AND HELPING IT APPEAR MORE INTEGRAL TO THE ROOM. **Right:** IN FOYERS THAT OPEN ONTO SEVERAL LIVING AREAS OF A HOME, A CHECKERBOARD TILE ARRANGEMENT CAN MAKE THE TRANSITION FROM ONE ROOM TO ANOTHER TASTEFUL AND DYNAMIC, NO MATTER WHAT THE ORIENTATION. THIS SIMPLE TILE GRID OFFERS A CLEAR-CUT SEPARATION BETWEEN THE LIVING ROOM AND DINING ROOM, AND PROMISES AN EQUALLY DRAMATIC VIEW FROM OTHER VANTAGE POINTS SUCH AS THE FRONT DOOR, DINING ROOM, AND UPSTAIRS LANDING.

Opposite: LIKE THE PROVERBIAL RED CARPET ROLLED OUT FOR DIGNITARIES, A BEAUTIFUL FLOOR CAN ELEVATE THE SPIRITS AND INFER STATUS IN EVEN ORDINARY SETTINGS. HERE, TRIANGLES OF POLISHED MARBLE COME TOGETHER IN A BOLD KALEIDOSCOPIC COMPOSITION. SUNLIGHT SPILLING THROUGH A LOW WINDOW INTO THIS GALLERYLIKE SETTING HIGHLIGHTS THE FLOOR'S NATURAL BEAUTY SO THAT LITTLE OTHER FURNISHINGS OR ART ARE NEEDED. **Below:** BEAUTIFUL AND MORE PRACTICAL THAN CARPETING, POLISHED MARBLE TILES IN A DEEP, MYSTERIOUS GREEN HUE TURN A LONG, NARROW HALL INTO A LUXURIOUS PALACE CORRIDOR. THE EVEN, SQUARE TILES DRAW THE EYE TOWARD A DISTANT VANISHING POINT, CREATING A SENSE OF ADVENTURE IN THIS DRAMATIC PASSAGEWAY. ONCE THE JOURNEY IS BEGUN, THE UNIQUE VEINING ON INDIVIDUAL TILES OFFERS CONTINUALLY CHANGING SCENERY ALONG THE WAY.

Above: TILE DESIGNS FROM THE COMMERCIAL ESTABLISHMENTS PATRONIZED BY EARLIER GENERATIONS CAN CREATE EXCITING PERIOD DECOR IN TODAY'S HOME. THIS BAR AREA TOOK A FANCIFUL SPIN BY INCORPORATING SODA FOUNTAIN SWIVEL STOOLS AT ITS ART DECO COUNTER. THE THREE-COLOR CERAMIC-TILE FLOOR LENDS AN AUTHENTICALLY CLASSY TOUCH, ALTERNATING WHITE AND BLACK OCTAGONAL TILES WITH SMALL BURGUNDY KEY TILES. GUESTS VIEW A DIFFERENT PATTERN IN THE SAME COLORS AS THEY CROSS THE COLUMN-FLANKED THRESHOLD.

Below: COMBINING THE BEAUTY OF HARDWOOD WITH THE PRACTICALITY OF TILE IN THIS OPEN-PLAN KITCHEN PROVIDED A STUNNING SOLUTION TO A REMODELING DILEMMA. SINCE HARDWOOD DOES NOT STAND UP PARTICULARLY WELL TO MESSY DRIPS AND SPILLS, TILES COME TO THE RESCUE UNDER THE WORK ISLAND, WHERE MOST OF THE COOKING AND EATING OCCURS. THE WHITE TILED AREA, WITH ITS BLUE CHECKERED BORDER, NOT ONLY PROVIDES AN EASY-TO-CLEAN SURFACE BUT ADDS DECORATIVE CHARM AS WELL, AESTHETICALLY SETTING OFF THE ISLAND FROM THE HARDWOOD SEA. **Opposite:** LIKE WILDFLOWERS SCATTERED ACROSS A FIELD, SMALL, MILKY WHITE KEY TILES SPROUT UP ON A PROVINCIAL KITCHEN'S TERRA-COTTA FLOOR. TWO SIZES OF TERRA-COTTA TILE, BOTH SQUARE IN SHAPE, ARE THE SECRET TO THIS SIMPLE BUT CHARMING LAYOUT THAT ESCHEWS A RIGID GRID FORMATION.

Above: A GALLEY-STYLE KITCHEN THAT TURNS A CORNER AT ONE END GETS A HAND DIRECTING TRAFFIC FLOW FROM A GROUP OF BRIGHT PURPLE FLOOR TILES. THE HIGHLY ARTISTIC TILES, EACH ONE HAND-DECORATED, STAND OUT IN THE LIGHT-TONED, MONOCHROMATIC KITCHEN AND MAKE ITS LAYOUT MORE READILY APPARENT. DISAPPEARING OUT OF SIGHT BEHIND A CABINET, THE PURPLE TILES ALSO INJECT AN AURA OF MYSTERY, HINTING THAT THERE IS MORE TO THIS KITCHEN AROUND THE CORNER.

Opposite: IN THIS LARGE BARN THAT HAS BEEN CONVERTED INTO A YEAR-ROUND HOME, A UTILITARIAN QUARRY-TILE FLOOR PUTS HOBBIES AND PASTIMES ON A SOLID FOOTING. INSTALLED PARTLY FOR ITS SOLAR PROPERTIES, THE FLOOR CAN BE SWEPT CLEAN AFTER SESSIONS AT THE WEAVING LOOM AND CAN WITHSTAND OCCASIONAL SPATTERS OF PAINT FROM ARTISTS AT THE EASEL. **Right:** IN KEEPING WITH THIS HOME'S SPANISH COLONIAL DECOR, A LARGE FORMAL DINING ROOM IS PAVED WITH MEXICAN CLAY TILES. INDIVIDUALLY SHAPED AND CUT BY HAND, THE BAKED TILES MANIFEST SUBTLE COLOR VARIATIONS THAT ADD TO THEIR AUTHENTICITY AND CHARM AS BUILDING MATERIALS. THE CONSPICUOUS ABSENCE OF A RUG BENEATH THE DINING TABLE AND CHAIRS ALLOWS THE TILES' ROUGH AND SOMEWHAT IRREGULAR SURFACE TO BE FULLY APPRECIATED.

Below: HERE, AN ANCIENT SPIRALED CHAIN DESIGN IS RENDERED MORE VISIBLE BY THE USE OF BLACK AND RUST TILES AGAINST A CREAMY YELLOW BACKGROUND. UNLIKE PERFECTLY SQUARE TILES, WHICH ARE LAID OUT IN A GRID, SMALLER, IRREGULAR MOSAIC TILES CAN BE ARRANGED IN SWIRLING AND CIRCULAR LINES FOR ENDLESS DESIGN AND COLOR POSSIBILITIES. BORDER DESIGNS OF THIS TYPE ARE MOST EFFECTIVE ALONG LENGTHY, UNBROKEN STRETCHES, WHERE THE MOTION AND RHYTHM OF THE DESIGN CAN GAIN SOME MOMENTUM.

Opposite: THE COLOR CHOSEN FOR A TILE FLOOR IS A POWERFUL MOOD DETERMINER, CAPABLE OF CONJURING UP A VARIETY OF LANDSCAPES, FROM A MOSSY KNOLL TO THE DESERT FLOOR. HERE, IN AN ENCLOSED PATIO, A BLUE TILE FLOOR SUGGESTS THE DISTANT OCEAN OR A MOUNTAIN LAKE.

Above: A GEOMETRIC BORDER IS A CLASSIC DECORATIVE TOOL FOR GIVING SOME FLAIR TO A FLOOR EXPANSE. CUTTING IN ON A WHITE, HEXAGONAL-TILE FLOOR, THIS GROUP OF TAUPE AND WHITE SQUARE TILES INTRODUCES A BORDER RESEMBLING THOSE FOUND ON ANCIENT GREEK ARTIFACTS. THE ROOM'S OVERALL NEUTRAL PALETTE ENSURES THAT THE BORDER, ONLY PARTIALLY IN VIEW HERE, RECEIVES DUE ATTENTION AS AN INTEGRAL PART OF THE DECOR.

Opposite: IMPRESSIVELY LARGE, DIMENSIONED RECTANGLES OF UNPOLISHED GRANITE IMPART A SENSE OF STRENGTH, PERMANENCE, AND SOLIDITY TO THIS ENTRYWAY.

Below: FOR THE DINING ROOM OF THIS COUNTRY HOME, THE DECORATING BYWORDS WERE SIMPLICITY AND CRAFTSMANSHIP. IN THE SEARCH FOR NATURAL, HONEST MATERIALS, REAL SLATE TILES AND RICHLY CRAFTED WOOD FURNITURE ENTERED THE PICTURE AS COMPATIBLE PARTNERS, TURNING A DREAMED-FOR ROOM INTO A REALITY.

Above: LARGE SQUARES OF DIMENSIONED STONE, SUITABLE FOR BOTH INDOOR AND OUTDOOR FLOORS, MAKE THE TRANSITION BETWEEN A CONTEMPORARY LIVING ROOM AND AN OPEN-AIR COURTYARD PRACTICALLY SEAMLESS. INDOORS, THE STONE'S HARD, SOPHISTICATED EDGE IS SOFTENED BY THE INTRODUCTION OF A DESIGNER AREA RUG AND UPHOLSTERED FURNISHINGS. OUTDOORS, THE DEEP GRAY COLOR APPEARS COOL AND MOIST NEXT TO THE GARDEN'S IVY-COVERED WALLS. TO MAINTAIN THE TOWN HOUSE'S ARCHITECTURAL INTEGRITY, THE SAME STONE IS USED IN THE UPSTAIRS BEDROOM.

First Impressions

In the rooms used to greet and entertain guests—entry halls, living rooms, and dining rooms—the decor is often glimpsed, like the stage set during a movie, through a whirl of dialogue, hugs, and familiar social exchanges. The all-important first impression is both swift and subliminal, reflecting more how people feel when they are in a room than what the room actually contains. Tiles can contribute greatly to that all-enveloping decorative aura called ambience. Covering large surface areas or showing up as decorative accents, they can convey in an instant whether a room is formal and well-ordered, relaxed and casual, or adventurous and artistic.

Far from being uninspiring, tile options for a home's living and entertainment areas include dimensioned stone, such as marble and granite, terra-cotta clay tiles with either rough or glazed surfaces, and ceramic tiles in colors and finishes far beyond the dreams of yesteryear's modest kitchen and bath offerings. The photographs in this section illustrate how these and other types of tile can enliven a home's public areas to make family and guests feel comfortable and at home. Used to enhance fireplaces, floors, ceilings, and a host of other architectural elements, tiles extend their own version of hospitality to residents and visitors alike.

Opposite: Upstaged by a towering ceiling and large expanses of window glass, the freestanding fireplace in this two-story living room originally had trouble maintaining its status as the room's focal point. A tiled fireplace surround came to the rescue by visually expanding the fireplace's width and height and by echoing on a more intimate scale the contours of the dynamic arched window. **Above:** Decorative tiles can be used outside a residence to identify the street address. Simple embellishments, these helpful tiles provide a welcoming and personal greeting to all who visit. Here, such tiles add much character and charm to the exterior of a Southwestern hacienda and suggest that similar authentic touches lie beyond the threshold.

Below: Whether welcoming one visitor or many, the classic black-and-white marble floor of this elegant reception foyer buzzes with excitement. Instead of the predictable checkerboard arrangement, the tiles take some interesting twists and turns that highlight the room's dimensions and furniture placement. Potted palms and a floral centerpiece help soften the tiles' angular shapes and make the polished sheen seem less austere. **Opposite:** In a pattern that mimics descending stair treads, a line of diamonds runs point to point around the edge of an entry hall's marble floor. Viewed from an upstairs landing, the diamonds heighten the drama of this two-story entry by defining the hall's borders. This same technique can be used on any floors that would benefit from bolder definition, particularly those in open floor plans where one room flows indiscriminately into another.

Above: When people's lives become busy or rushed, the role that a serene, tasteful entry hall can play in calming jangled nerves and restoring perspective should not be underestimated. While the white marble of this tiled entryway floor suggests permanence and stability, the dark veining, with its soothing, swirling fluidity, prevents the surface from seeming too austere. Combined, these components work together to help ground and comfort those who arrive.

Opposite: IN THE SPACIOUS ENTRY HALL OF THIS SOUTHWESTERN HOME, GUESTS ALWAYS WARM TO THE SIGHT OF FESTIVE TILED STAIR RISERS, NO TWO ALIKE. PAVED WITH LARGE MEXICAN TERRA-COTTA TILES, THE ENTIRE ENTRY EXUDES A WARM GLOW BY DAY OR NIGHT. JUST OUTSIDE THE FRONT DOOR, DEEP COBALT BLUE GLAZED TILES DROP IN ON THE TERRA-COTTA SURFACE, ADDING A GLASSY SHEEN THAT HELPS DEFINE THE INDOOR AND OUTDOOR AREAS. **Below:** ADJACENT TO A CARVED MARBLE DOOR FRAME, THIS COLORFUL MOSAIC PANEL FURTHER DEFINES THE HALLWAY ENTRANCE TO A LIVING ROOM. THE INTRICATE DESIGN, WHICH INCLUDES NATURAL LEAF MOTIFS AS WELL AS AN INTERLOCKING CELTIC KNOT, INVITES CLOSE INSPECTION FROM ALL WHO LINGER IN THE ENTRYWAY.

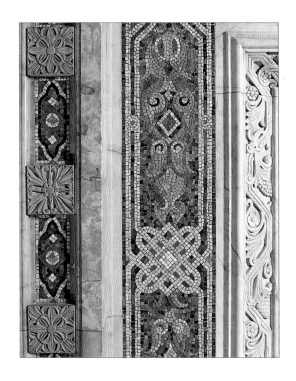

Above: IN A ROOM USED FOR ENTERTAINING GUESTS, A WET BAR CAN CUT DOWN ON TRIPS TO AND FROM THE KITCHEN FOR REFRESHMENTS. HERE, A COUNTER AND BACKSPLASH ARE PROTECTED BY TILES THAT TIE IN WITH THE ROOM'S SOUTHWESTERN DECOR. TO AVOID DISRUPTING THE COLORFUL DESIGN, THE OUTLET AND LIGHT-SWITCH PLATES LAID OVER THE TILES HAVE BEEN PAINTED SO THAT THEY CONTINUE THE STEPPED BORDER PATTERN.

Below: WHEN MARBLE TILES ARE APPLIED TO BOTH THE FLOOR OF AN ENTRY HALL AND THE FORMAL ROOMS THAT LIE BEYOND IT, THE ENTIRE SPACE CAN BE VISUALLY EXPANDED. HERE, A SLEEK, OPEN LOOK WAS CREATED BY USING A PALE GRAY MARBLE FLOOR THAT FLOWS FROM THE HALL INTO THE DINING ROOM TO UNITE THESE TWO AREAS. **Opposite:** THE SAME DECORATING TRICK OF USING LIKE TILES TO LINK ROOMS WITHIN A HOME CAN BE PERFORMED TO VISUALLY JOIN AN INTERIOR SPACE WITH THE EXTERIOR. PAVING THE FLOOR OF THIS ENTRY FOYER, CRISP DIMENSIONED-STONE TILES THAT WOULD LOOK EQUALLY AT HOME ON A PATIO BLUR THE DISTINCTION BETWEEN OUTDOORS AND INDOORS. ALTHOUGH THE FOYER TILES DIFFER SLIGHTLY FROM THOSE ON THE GARDEN PATH IN TERMS OF SHAPE AND DIRECTION, THE SIMILARITY IN COLOR AND MATERIAL CREATES THE OVERALL ILLUSION OF A SINGLE, CONTINUOUS SPACE.

Above: IN LONG, OPEN HALLWAYS, MARBLE FLOORING IS UNSURPASSED FOR EXTENDING A BEAUTIFUL VISTA. THE ORANGY RED MARBLE CHOSEN FOR THIS FOYER CONTINUES DOWN AN ADJACENT HALL, LEADING THE EYE ON AN UNINTERRUPTED JOURNEY TO THE CARPETED LIVING ROOM AT THE REAR OF THE HOME. DESPITE ITS EXQUISITE COLOR, THE LARGE EXPANSE OF MARBLE DOESN'T OVERPOWER THE SPACE, BUT RATHER ANCHORS IT. BLACK KEY TILES APPEAR LESS PROMINENT THAN THEY DO AGAINST WHITE MARBLE, ADDING TO THE ENTRY'S UNDERSTATED ELEGANCE.

Opposite: PROVIDING AN UNEXPECTED TOUCH TO A COZY DINING AREA, THIS CERAMIC TILE CEILING WAS INSPIRED BY EUROPEAN MANOR HOUSE KITCHENS THAT WERE EXTENSIVELY TILED AS A SAFEGUARD AGAINST FIRE.

Below: FINDING A CREATIVE USE FOR TILES IN AN ENTRY HALL CAN PROVIDE A GUEST WITH AN INNOVATIVE GREETING THAT WILL LEAVE A LASTING IMPRESSION. HERE, BLUE-AND-WHITE DELFT TILES ADORN A WOODEN BOX OF PINECONES THAT MIGHT OTHERWISE BLEND IN WITH THE BROWN, WOOD FLOOR AND GO UNNOTICED. THE COLORS ON THE TILES SERVE AS A LINK WITH THE STRATEGICALLY PLACED BLUE-AND-WHITE CHINA PLATE ON THE TABLE ABOVE, THEREBY ENCOURAGING THE EYE TO TRAVEL FREELY BETWEEN THESE TWO LEVELS.

Above: IMPARTING A FORMAL AMBIENCE THAT BELIES THEIR PRACTICALITY, THE BLACK AND WHITE MARBLE TILES ADORNING THIS ENTRY HALL EASILY STAND UP TO DRIPPING UMBRELLAS AND WET BOOTS. LAID ON THE DIAGONAL, THE TILES FORM A SYMMETRICAL DIAMOND DESIGN THAT TAKES ADVANTAGE OF THE AREA'S SQUARE PROPORTIONS. BLACK EDGING TILES LINE THE PERIMETER, ACCENTUATING THE NEAT, TRIM LOOK.

Opposite: A COLORFUL, TILED SURROUND CAN INJECT SOME WELCOME PERSONALITY INTO WHAT WOULD OTHERWISE BE AN ORDINARY AND EASILY OVERLOOKED FIREPLACE. THIS HOMEY LIVING ROOM PULLED OUT ALL THE STOPS, ASSEMBLING A CASUAL, UNINHIBITED MIX OF BOTH WARM AND COOL COLORS, FROM WHICH A GROUP OF BRILLIANT TURQUOISE TILES IN THE FIREPLACE SURROUND POPS OUT. THE TURQUOISE HUE HELPS THE UNUSUAL TILEWORK HOLD ITS OWN AMONG THE ROOM'S MANY OTHER COMPELLING FURNISHINGS AND DECORATIVE OBJECTS. **Above, left:** ESCHEWING MACHINE PRECISION AND SHINY GLAZES FOR A SIMPLE MATTE TEXTURE, THE TILES OF AN ARTS AND CRAFTS FIREPLACE DISPLAY THE QUIET, UNDERSTATED BEAUTY THAT CAN EMERGE WHEN OBJECTS ARE MADE BY HAND. THESE TILES HAVE BEEN CRAFTED WITH PARTICULAR FIREPLACE DIMENSIONS IN MIND, AS EVIDENCED BY THE GENTLY SWIRLING ART NOUVEAU INLAY. **Above, right:** A WELCOMING, COZY FIRE APPEARS EVEN BRIGHTER WHEN THE FIREPLACE SURROUND IS A DARK OR SOMBER COLOR. HERE, FOREST GREEN TILES ENCASE A FREESTANDING FIREPLACE, FRAMING THE DANCING FLAMES WITHIN. ON THE PRACTICAL SIDE, THE DARK TILES ACTUALLY HELP KEEP THE ROOM WARM BY RETAINING HEAT FROM THE FIRE AND RADIATING IT OUT INTO THE ROOM. IN LIEU OF A HEARTH, SMALL CERAMIC TILES PROTECT THE IMMEDIATE FLOOR AREA FROM STRAY SPARKS.

Opposite: IN AN ARTSY LIVING ROOM DECORATED WITH PAINTINGS, WALL STENCILING, AND ECLECTIC FURNISHINGS, A TRADITIONAL BRICK FIREPLACE MAY SIMPLY BE TOO PROSAIC. HERE, A UNIQUE AND HIGHLY AFFORDABLE FINISH WAS CREATED USING CHIPS OF BROKEN TILE IN A RAINBOW OF COLORS. THE IRREGULAR SHARDS FIT TOGETHER LIKE THE TILES IN A MOSAIC, FORMING A TOTALLY RANDOM DESIGN EXCEPT FOR A SMALL BROWN PINWHEEL THAT APPEARS ABOVE THE FIREPLACE OPENING. THE COLORS ECHO THOSE USED THROUGHOUT THE ROOM, AND AS A RESULT, THE FIREPLACE PULLS TOGETHER THE ENTIRE ECLECTIC DECOR.

Above: TINY DOTS, SQUIGGLES, AND PATCHES OF COLOR FLUTTER ACROSS THE SURFACE OF THIS FIREPLACE SURROUND LIKE A SHOWER OF AIRBORNE CONFETTI. THE COLORFUL PIECES ARE ACTUALLY BITS OF BROKEN TILE SUSPENDED IN PLASTER, A TECHNIQUE THAT BYPASSES THE CONVENTIONAL—AND TIME-CONSUMING—ASPECTS OF TILE SETTING AND GROUTING. MORE FREE-FORM WITH GREATER BETWEEN-TILE SPACES THAN A TRADITIONAL MOSAIC, THE UNCONVENTIONAL COMPOSITION EXHIBITS A LIVELY INTERCHANGE BETWEEN SHAPES AND COLORS THAT AROUSES CURIOSITY AND DRAWS ATTENTION.

Tiles in the Kitchen

Tiles and cooking go hand in hand. Easily wiped clean and resistant to heat and water, tiles are the logical choice for kitchen countertops, backsplashes, stove alcoves, and floors. Tiles perform their kitchen chores quietly and efficiently, catching splashes and spatters without being prompted and receiving hot roasting pans with nary a scorch mark.

While utility has long been the express function of kitchen tiles, the broad range of tiles currently being designed and produced to enhance kitchen decor demonstrates the importance of their aesthetic contribution as well. Tiles are tactile decorative elements, capable of evoking a sense of place and time in a kitchen just as readily as they do in other areas of the home. Choices range from polished marble, for a sleek, elegant floor

or backsplash, to hand-painted ceramic, for a cozy, provincial kitchen that provides a farmhouse ambience. Working in tandem with kitchen cabinets and appliances, which add their own distinctive look to the overall decorating mix, tiles can forge a personality for a kitchen that is as unique and individual as the people who use it.

The photographs in this section show a range of kitchens that incorporate tiles into their design with decorative as well as functional purposes in mind. Some of the kitchens use tiles sparingly, employing them as essential accents, while others spread them lavishly across counters, walls, and floors. Each example provides valuable ideas regarding tile materials, sizes, colors, and arrangements that can be adapted to kitchens everywhere.

Opposite: Reminiscent of nineteenth-century New England stenciling, the delicate, graphic leaf pattern on these backsplash tiles adds decorative variety and traditional interest to this highly efficient contemporary kitchen. On the floor, solid black tiles anchor the room while giving the white cabinetry a floating appearance. **Above:** Defying convention with its unusual composition, this backsplash gives helpers at the kitchen sink a geology lesson whenever they look up from washing vegetables or scrubbing dishes. Set within a frame of white tile shards, a slab of gray mottled granite shares its natural beauty while protecting the wall from water droplets. Although ordinary square ceramic tiles are used to complete the unusual backsplash, their rows are staggered to maintain an offbeat look and avoid a strict grid.

Right: A STUDY IN CONTRASTS, THIS STUNNING, CONTEMPORARY KITCHEN TEMPERS ITS STAINLESS STEEL CABINETS AND APPLIANCES WITH SUBTLY VEINED PINK AND RUSSET MARBLE. THE USE OF LARGE FLOOR TILES IN THE CENTRAL, MAIN AREA OF THE THE ROOM COMBINED WITH THE PLACEMENT OF SMALLER ONES AROUND THE PERIMETER CREATES THE APPEARANCE OF A LARGE AREA RUG, A LOOK THAT IS EMPHASIZED BY THE BORDER OF DIAMOND-SHAPED TILES. SEPARATING THE LARGE TILES FROM THE WALKWAY OF SMALL TILES, THIS BORDER ECHOES THE LONG, NARROW HARLEQUIN DIAMONDS COVERING THE BACK-SPLASH ON THE FAR WALL.

Above: WHEN THE EXTRA STORAGE A CABINET PROVIDES IS ESSENTIAL BUT THE TILE WALL BEHIND IT IS TOO BEAUTIFUL TO COVER UP, THE SEE-THROUGH APPROACH MAY PROVE TO BE A UNIQUE COMPROMISE. AFTER THE NARROW BACKBOARD WAS REMOVED AND THIS STOCK CABINET WAS REMOUNTED ON THE WALL, ITS CLEAR GLASS DOORS BECAME AN INSTANT WINDOW TO THE AQUA TILES BEHIND IT. THE COLORED TILES SERVE AS AN ATTRACTIVE BACKDROP FOR THE ASSORTED DISHES AND GLASSWARE.

Opposite: ONE WAY TO AVOID PREDICTABILITY IN A KITCHEN DESIGN IS TO CHOOSE UNUSUAL, EYE-CATCHING TILES FOR THE BACKSPLASH. IN THIS CONTEMPORARY KITCHEN, BLOND WOOD DRAWERS BELOW THE COUNTER AND SMOKY GRAY CABINETS ABOVE ARE LINKED BY SUBTLY SHADED YET COLORFUL TILES, EACH ONE BEARING A DIFFERENT TEXTURED DESIGN. SET AGAINST NEUTRAL COLORS AND LOCATED ABOVE THE COUNTER, THESE TILES REVEAL THEIR AESTHETIC POTENTIAL TO THE FULLEST AND INVITE CLOSE EXAMINATION OF THEIR INTRICATE CRAFTSMANSHIP. **Below:** TILES DO NOT HAVE TO INUNDATE A KITCHEN IN ORDER TO BE USEFUL. INSTEAD, THEY CAN BE USED AS SUBTLE, PRACTICAL ACCENTS. HERE, A SLATE TILE COUNTERTOP BREAKS UP THE MONOTONY OF AN ALL-WOOD KITCHEN AND ITS ALL-WHITE CABINETS, WHILE AT THE SAME TIME COORDINATING BEAUTIFULLY WITH THE PANELED DOORS AND BRASS HARDWARE. HEAT-PROOF AND EASY TO CLEAN, A TILE COUNTERTOP IS A PERFECT MEANS FOR ATTAINING PRACTICALITY WITHOUT SACRIFICING BEAUTY.

Above: ALTHOUGH WALL-MOUNTED, ABOVE-COUNTER CABINETS THAT EXTEND ALL THE WAY TO THE CEILING CAN PROVIDE VITAL STORAGE IN A KITCHEN, THEY CAN ALSO LOOM UNPLEASANTLY OVERHEAD. TO DRAW ATTENTION BACK DOWN TO THE COUNTERTOP WORK AREA IN THIS EAT-IN KITCHEN, A BOLD BACKSPLASH WAS CREATED USING BRIGHT BLUE-GREEN CERAMIC TILES. THEIR MID-WALL PLACEMENT INDUCES THE SAME NATURALLY SOOTHING EFFECT AS GAZING ON THE SEA OR HORIZON.

Below: RECESSED WITHIN A FULLY TILED ALCOVE, THIS COUNTERTOP RANGE IS TRANSFORMED INTO A SELF-CONTAINED COOKING CENTER. THE CHEERFUL, BLUE-AND-GOLD MAJOLICA TILES COVER THE ENTIRE INTERIOR, INCLUDING THE SHALLOW BUILT-IN SIDE SHELVES, AND PREVENT THE ALCOVE FROM APPEARING DARK AND SHADOWY. PRACTICAL AS WELL AS BEAUTIFUL, THE TILE SURFACE WIPES CLEAN WITH A DAMP SPONGE AT THE END OF EACH COOKING SESSION.

Opposite: RISING LIKE A MONUMENT TO HISTORY, AN UPDATED COOKING HEARTH IS COVERED, FLOOR TO CEILING, WITH DELFT TILES THAT ARE ARRANGED MUCH AS THEY WOULD HAVE BEEN IN A SEVENTEENTH-CENTURY DUTCH HOME. WHILE THE VARIOUS TILES CREATE A STRIKING SURFACE OVERALL, THE INDIVIDUAL PICTURE TILES, SHOWING GEOGRAPHIC LOCATIONS, SAILING SHIPS, AND PEOPLE, ARE ALSO MEANT TO BE ADMIRED UP CLOSE. WHITE INSETS IN THE RED CLAY FLOOR ECHO THE NEAT, BOXY CONFIGURATION OF THE WALL TILES WHILE UPHOLDING THE HEARTH'S DOMINANT STATURE.

Above: TUCKED INTO A TILE-EDGED ALCOVE, AN OLD-FASHIONED KITCHEN RANGE IS PAMPERED WITH STYLE. PRETTIER THAN BLACK, THE TILES' DARK COBALT BLUE COLOR STILL PROVIDES CRISP CONTRAST AGAINST THE OFF-WHITE WALL, THEREBY CALLING ATTENTION TO THE ALCOVE AND ALERTING PEOPLE TO BE CAREFUL AROUND THE POTENTIALLY HOT STOVE. THE SLENDER DELINEATION OF THE ALCOVE OPENING SUITS THE SIMPLE UTILITARIAN BEAUTY OF THE STOVE WITHOUT OVERPOWERING IT.

Opposite: WHEN SELECTING HAND-PAINTED TILES, LAYING THEM OUT EDGE TO EDGE IS ESSENTIAL TO SEE HOW THE PATTERNS INTERCONNECT OVER A LARGER SURFACE. EACH ONE OF THE DELICATE, EVENLY SPACED PATTERNS ON THIS KITCHEN BACKSPLASH IS FORMED WHEN THE CORNERS OF FOUR TILES INTERSECT. ON SOME OF THE TILES, THE CORNER DESIGNS HAVE BEEN OMITTED IN FAVOR OF OTHER OPTIONS, SUCH AS THE COLORFUL PARROTS AND VASE. THE TILES USED TO CREATE THESE LARGER NOVELTY PICTURES COST A LITTLE MORE, BUT THEY CAN BE USED AS GENEROUSLY OR AS SPARINGLY AS A BUDGET OR PERSONAL PREFERENCE ALLOWS. **Below:** MIMICKING THE PAINTED TILES THAT ADORNED LATE NINETEENTH-CENTURY CAFÉS, RAILROAD STATIONS, AND DEPARTMENT STORES, A MONKEY-AND-HARE TABLEAU PROVIDES FANCIFUL SCENERY FOR DINERS AT A KITCHEN SNACK BAR. THE STONE ARCHES ON EITHER SIDE OF THE RANGE HOOD ARE ACTUALLY A TROMPE L'OEIL EFFECT, CREATED BY PAINTING A REALISTIC DESIGN ON INDIVIDUAL FLAT TILES.

Above: FOR COOKS INCLINED TO KEEP THEIR ROPES OF GARLIC AND ONIONS IN COOL, DRY STORAGE INSTEAD OF HANGING THEM IN A HOT KITCHEN, PICTURE TILES CAN OFFER A WORTHY VISUAL SUBSTITUTE. FRAMED WITH NARROW, BLACK BORDER TILES, THE IMAGES ON THE BACK WALL OF THIS COOKING ALCOVE DISPLAY ALL THE DETAIL OF NINETEENTH-CENTURY ENGRAVINGS. THEY PROVIDE A MORE INTERESTING VIEW FOR THE COOK THAN DO PLAIN GRAY TILES, YET THEY ARE JUST AS EASY TO WIPE CLEAN. RECESSED BULBS WITHIN THE ALCOVE SHED LIGHT ON THE ARTWORK AS WELL AS THE COOKTOP.

Above, left: CHOSEN TO MATCH A FAVORITE COLOR SCHEME OR TO REFLECT A SPECIAL INTEREST OR HOBBY, HAND-PAINTED, ONE-OF-A-KIND TILES ARE THE PERFECT WAY TO CUSTOMIZE A KITCHEN OR BAR. ALTHOUGH COMMISSIONED DESIGNS CAN BE QUITE LAVISH, SOME EXTENDING OVER AN ENTIRE COUNTER OR WALL, EVEN SMALL VIGNETTES, SUCH AS THE AMICABLE WINE BOTTLE AND FRUIT BASKET SHOWN HERE, CAN BESTOW CHARM AND PERSONALITY. WORKED INTO THE EDGE OF A BACKSPLASH OR COUNTER, THEY CAN GIVE PLAIN TILED SURFACES AN ELEMENT OF SURPRISE AND DELIGHT. **Above, right:** AWKWARD TO REACH, THE INNER CORNERS OF KITCHEN COUNTERS TEND TO BE DEAD SPOTS, ACCUMULATING SELDOM USED APPLIANCES IN A CLUTTERED JUMBLE. TO ENSURE THAT A CORNER OF THIS COUNTER NEVER BECOMES DULL, TILES SHOWING A BASKET OF FLOWERS HAVE BEEN INCORPORATED IN THE BACKSPLASH. THE PRETTY ADDITION HAS SO BRIGHTENED THE AREA THAT THE COOK NOW USES THIS SPACE TO REST CULINARY CREATIONS UNTIL SERVING TIME. **Opposite:** LIKE THAT OF A GRAND BARONIAL MANOR HOUSE, THIS AMPLY APPOINTED KITCHEN REVELS IN ITS LUXURIOUSLY TILED SURFACES. NOT ONLY DO TILES COVER THE HOOD, WALLS, AND ISLAND COUNTERTOP OF THIS KITCHEN, BUT THEY PROVIDE SPOTS OF COLOR ON THE DARK CABINETS AS WELL. THE PREDOMINANTLY WHITE, BLUE, AND YELLOW TILES ARE CHARMINGLY PROVINCIAL, SPELLING OUT THE FRENCH NAMES FOR VARIOUS FOODS THROUGHOUT THE KITCHEN.

Making a Splash

Bathrooms, spas, and pools are places where water and tiles meet with splashy decorative results. Constantly coming into contact with water, these areas require waterproof surfaces, and tiles rise to the occasion. Capable of creating everything from a flowery, provincial bathroom to a sleek, ultramodern spa, tiles provide ambience while satisfying practical needs.

In the world of bathroom decor, the tile is king. Just about every surface in a bathroom—floor, shower stall, tub surround, counter, and lower wall—must be made waterproof. The need in bathrooms for broad expanses of tiling makes walls and floors ready canvases for creative designs and color combinations. Mirrors and counter edges cry out to be adorned with innovative border tiles. While the preferred tile for bathrooms continues to be shiny glazed ceramic, slightly textured surfaces, which help prevent slipping, and marble are gaining ground.

In spas and pool areas, the utilitarian and aesthetic features of tiles combine to create inviting, refreshing aquatic retreats. Indoor spas, with their proximity to a home's main living areas, are prime candidates for creative tilework that coordinates with the overall decor while providing essential waterproofing. Swimming pools show off tiles with mesmerizing results, refracting and reflecting the colors and patterns through the water's gentle, perpetual undulation.

The following pages reveal bathrooms, spas, and pools that go beyond the usual, predictable tile installations to experiment with color, mood, and surface texture. Each design offers an example of how to make these areas of the home comfortably suited to individual needs, tastes, and preferences.

Opposite: Created from a palette of candy-colored pastels, this extraordinary assemblage of basic squares and rectangles puts a new spin on the phrase "fully tiled bath." The tiles are manufactured in proportional sizes to ensure continuous, even grid lines when tiles of different sizes appear next to one another. **Above:** Basic white ceramic tiles are often the backbone of a precisely engineered master bathroom. Here, small, black square tiles and a thin, black edging tile add a dressy touch above twin arched mirrors.

Below: WHEN A BATHROOM'S MOST INTERESTING FEATURES ARE ARCHITECTURAL, TILES SHOULD BE USED TO ENHANCE RATHER THAN CONFUSE THE DETAILS. HERE, A STRAIGHTFORWARD, PREDICTABLE GRID, FORMED BY DEEP GRAY TILES SET WITH WHITE GROUT, SHOWS OFF THE UNUSUAL ANGLED PLANES OF A TOWEL STORAGE AREA AND AN EIGHT-DRAWER VANITY BASE. A BRIGHTER COLOR COULD MAKE THE SKEWED SURFACES SEEM JARRING, BUT THE SOMBER HUE IMBUES THEM WITH QUIET SOPHISTICATION. **Opposite:** IN A FLAWLESS, VISUALLY SEAMLESS INSTALLATION, POLISHED MARBLE FLOOR TILES CONTINUE UP THE SIDES OF A TUB SURROUND AND LINE THE KICK SPACES UNDER THE MATCHING VANITIES, MAKING THIS BATHING AREA IMPERVIOUS TO DRIPS AND SPLASHES. THE SMOOTH, COOL MARBLE IS REFRESHINGLY THERAPEUTIC TO BARE FEET, AS WELL AS SOOTHING TO THE EYE.

Above: A ROOM WITHIN A ROOM, THIS GLASS-WALLED SHOWER STALL IS TILED ON THE FLOOR AND ON ONE SIDE TO CONCEAL THE DRAIN AND WATER PIPES. THE TILES INSIDE THE STALL ARE A PLEASING AQUA SHADE SUGGESTIVE OF TROPICAL WATERS, WHILE THOSE ON THE BACK WALL OUTLINING THE SHOWER AREA ARE A BOLD BLACK THAT HELPS TO BRING OUT THE DARK VEINING ON THE WHITE MARBLE FLOOR.

Left: THIS TUB'S UNIQUE DESIGN OF COLORFUL BLOCKS IS CREATED FROM SMALL SQUARE TILES ARRANGED IN A GEOMETRIC MOSAIC. ECHOING THE RED AND YELLOW VANITY DOORS AND DRAWERS, THESE UPBEAT TILES GIVE THE BATHROOM A UNIFIED LOOK WHILE PROVIDING THE AREA WITH A PRACTICAL, WATER-RESISTANT SURFACE. **Above:** A SMALL BATHROOM IS THE PERFECT PLACE TO INDULGE IN A ZANY TILE DESIGN THAT WOULD BE TOO BOLD OR WILD ELSEWHERE IN THE HOUSE. TILES ARE THE MAIN CONTRIBUTORS TO THIS WORK OF ART; THEIR IRREGULAR SHAPES, DIAGONAL PLACEMENT, CUSTOM GLAZES, AND MIX OF BOLD AND SUBTLE COLORS PRODUCE A LIVELY COLLAGE. WITH A LITTLE IMAGINATION, A DYNAMIC ASSEMBLAGE SUCH AS THIS CAN BE CREATED INEXPENSIVELY BY USING BEAUTIFUL TILES THAT HAVE BEEN LEFT OVER FROM OTHER PROJECTS OR DISCONTINUED, AS THESE CAN OFTEN BE PURCHASED IN SMALL QUANTITIES AT A DISCOUNT.

Below: OFTEN CHOSEN TO MAKE A HALF-BATH OR SMALL BATHROOM APPEAR LARGER, PALE OR LIGHT-COLORED TILES RUN THE CONCURRENT RISK OF APPEARING BLAND AND UNINSPIRING. TO ADD COLOR AND TEXTURAL INTEREST TO THIS SMALL BATH, THREE DIFFERENT SCULPTED TILE BORDERS IN A DEEP GREEN COLOR WERE WORKED INTO THE BASIC PALE GRAY SCHEME. AS PART OF THE GENERAL STRATEGY TO KEEP THE EYE WANDERING ABOUT THE ROOM, A PEBBLE-TEXTURED FLOOR INTRODUCES ANOTHER GEOMETRIC PATTERN.

Above: INSTEAD OF OUTLINING THE MIRROR IN THIS BATHROOM WITH SPECIALLY SHAPED TILES, THE DESIGNER OPTED TO USE TILES OF THE EXACT SAME SHAPE AND COLOR ALL ACROSS THE WALL OF THE SINK AREA. TO ACHIEVE A BORDER EFFECT, HOWEVER, THE TILES IMMEDIATELY FRAMING THE MIRROR WERE DIFFERENTIATED BY THE ADDITION OF A SIMPLE GEOMETRIC DESIGN PLACED IN THE MIDDLE OF EACH. THIS SAME DESIGN APPEARS ABOVE THE BATH ON WHITE TILES THAT FORM A FRAME AROUND SMALLER BLACK TILES TO CREATE THE IMAGE OF A PAINTING HANGING ON THE WALL.

Above: THE GRAPHIC, GEOMETRIC QUALITY INHERENT IN CERAMIC TILE INSTALLATIONS IS WELL SUITED TO HIGHLIGHTING, OUTLINING, AND DELINEATING A BATHROOM'S PHYSICAL FEATURES AND AMENITIES. IN THIS MASTER BATHROOM, TWIN MIRRORS ARE EACH FRAMED WITH NAVY TILES, HELPING THEM STAND OUT AGAINST A SOFT GRAY BACKGROUND. THE LOWER EDGE OF EACH FRAME CONTINUES ALONG THE WALL, FORMING A CRISP LINE ALONG THE BACK OF THE VANITY AND MARKING THE BOTTOM SHELF OF A TILED NICHE USED FOR HAND TOWELS AND WASHCLOTHS. THE FRONT EDGE OF THE VANITY IS PROTECTED WITH ROUND-EDGED TRIM TILES, ALSO IN NAVY, WHICH CONTRAST AGAINST THE WHITE CABINETRY BELOW.

Below: THERE'S NO RULE THAT SAYS HIGH-TECH CHROME AND GLASS FIXTURES HAVE TO BE TEAMED WITH WHITE, BLACK, OR GRAY TILES TO LOOK SLEEK AND STREAMLINED. HERE, CHROME FIXTURES TAKE ON A LUSTROUS GLOW AGAINST A BACK-DROP OF TILES GLAZED IN WARM, EARTHY COLORS.

Above: WHEN NO COLOR IN PARTICULAR STANDS OUT AS THE PERFECT CHOICE FOR A BATHROOM REMODELING, A MULTICOLOR BORDER TILE MAY SUGGEST SOME POSSIBILITIES. THE SOUTHWESTERN BORDER TILE CHOSEN FOR THIS LIVELY FAMILY BATHROOM FEATURES A HOST OF PAINT-BOX COLORS, WITH HUES RANGING FROM ORANGE TO MAGENTA TO DEEP VIOLET. TILES FOR THE WALLS AND FLOOR WERE CHOSEN TO MATCH, AND ADDITIONAL COLORS WERE THROWN IN TO CREATE A VERITABLE COLOR FIESTA. PAINTED SOLID ORANGE, THE UPPER WALL GIVES THE EYE AN INTERMITTENT RESTING PLACE FROM THE DAZZLING DISPLAY BELOW.

Right: IN THIS EXTENSIVELY TILED BATHROOM, THE BORDERS AND BACKDROP HAVE ONLY ONE COLOR IN COMMON. AGAINST A SOLID BACKGROUND OF GREEN TILES, BLACK DIAMONDS BORDERED BY VIVID, MULTICOLOR SHAPES DELINEATE THE MIRROR AND THE EDGE OF THE VANITY, PROVIDING EXCITING GEOMETRIC CONTRAST AND COLOR. THE FEW SMALL, GREEN TRIANGLES WITHIN THE BORDERS ARE ALL THAT ARE NECESSARY TO LINK THE TILES TO THE SURROUNDING TILED SURFACES.

Below: JUMBLING UP AN ARRANGEMENT OF PATTERNED TILES IS ONE WAY TO KEEP AN ELEMENT OF SPONTANEITY IN A BATHROOM THAT'S USED EVERY DAY. VIEWED IMMEDIATELY UPON ENTERING THE ROOM, THE ZIGZAG BACKSPLASH BEHIND THE SINK SETS UP THE REASONABLE EXPECTATION THAT OTHER TILES IN THE ROOM WILL BE ARRANGED IN THE SAME CONFIGURATION. HOWEVER, THE SHOWER STALL TILES, WITH THEIR SENSE OF WILD ABANDON, ARE A WELCOME SURPRISE; THEY PREVENT THE ORDERLY AND GRACIOUSLY APPOINTED ROOM, COMPLETE WITH HANDSOME WOOD CABINET AND FULLY PLUMBED, OLD-FASHIONED SINK BASIN, FROM TAKING ITSELF TOO SERIOUSLY.

Opposite: HERE, HUNDREDS OF TINY TILES ASSEMBLED IN VARIOUS PATTERNS COVERING THE WALLS, CEILING, AND FLOOR SUGGEST THE RICH TILE-WORK TRADITION OF THE OTTOMAN EMPIRE. ALTHOUGH THE INDIVIDUAL TILES ARE SIMPLE IN BOTH SHAPE AND COLOR, THEIR SHEER PROFUSION COMBINED WITH THE DIZZYING EFFECT OF HAVING DIFFERENT PATTERNS DISPLAYED SIDE BY SIDE RENDERS THEM MAGNIFICENT.

Above: ON A CONTOURED SURFACE, SMALL TILES ARE BEST FOR YIELDING A SMOOTHER, MORE SATISFYING FINISH. IN THIS LARGE BATHROOM, A SEMICIRCULAR NICHE CREATED FOR A ROUND, CURTAINLESS SHOWER STALL IS LINED WITH THOUSANDS OF SMALL TILES. DRAWING ON A NEUTRAL PALETTE, THE TILES ARE ARRANGED INTO DELICATE DIAMOND DESIGNS, CROSSES, AND AT THE BOTTOM EDGE, ROLLING OCEAN WAVES. A DIMENSIONED-STONE FLOOR WITH RED KEY TILES PROTECTS THE AREA OUTSIDE THE SHALLOW SHOWER WELL FROM SPLASHES.

Opposite: ROMANTIC AND LIGHTHEARTED IN ITS DECORATING APPROACH, THIS BATHROOM INCORPORATES SEVERAL STYLES OF TILE THAT WORK TOGETHER BECAUSE OF THEIR SHARED MEDITERRANEAN HERITAGE. RISING UP FROM A TRADITIONAL CLAY TILE FLOOR ARE CERAMIC TILES, COLORED WITH A WATERY BLUE GLAZE AND SET ON THE DIAGONAL, AND MAJOLICA-STYLE PAINTED TILES. THE CHARMING DESIGNS INCLUDE A TOWERING VASE OF FLOWERS, A CAGED BIRD, AND GARLAND-WRAPPED COLUMNS, WHICH WHIMSICALLY FLANK THE ENTRANCE TO THE WATER CLOSET. **Below:** FILLED WITH LUXURIOUS TOUCHES, A MASTER BATH TAKES FULL ADVANTAGE OF ITS ARCHITECTURAL DESIGN. THE ARCHING GLASS ENCLOSURE GIVES THE TUB FULL EXPOSURE TO SUNLIGHT OR MOONLIGHT, WHILE A BLUE TILE FLOOR WASHES ACROSS THE ROOM AND UP THE SIDE OF THE TUB LIKE A BREAKING OCEAN WAVE. A SMALL, SHELL-SHAPED SINK IS INSET IN THE LONG, WHITE TILED COUNTER.

Above: DECORATIVE TILES CAN HELP ESTABLISH A THEME OR A MOOD JUST AS READILY AS WALLPAPER OR TEXTILES. IN THIS CHARMING POWDER ROOM, WHITE CERAMIC TILES WITH A FLORAL MOTIF LINE THE DADO, WHILE SOLID WHITE TILES SET WITH FLORAL KEY TILES PROTECT THE FLOOR. A FIRST STEP IN ENSURING THAT WALLPAPER AND TILE PATTERNS DON'T CLASH IS TO SELECT DIFFERENT-SIZE PATTERNS, SUCH AS THOSE SHOWN HERE.

Below: DELINEATING THE OUTER EDGE OF THIS SPA, A CHECKERED BAND CREATES A SATISFYING TRANSITION BETWEEN THE PINK INTERIOR AND THE DEEP TEAL FLOOR BEYOND. THE LARGE TILED AREA SURROUNDING THE SPA PROVIDES PLENTY OF SPACE FOR BATHERS TO DRY OFF.

Opposite: A DEEP SUNKEN SOAKING TUB WITH WHIRLPOOL JETS TURNS THE EVERYDAY AFFAIR OF BATHING INTO A LUXURIOUS EVENT. THE INTERIOR OF THIS TUB IS TASTEFULLY LINED WITH TINY MOSAIC TILES, SUGGESTVE OF AN ANCIENT ROMAN BATH.

Above: STEPS AWAY FROM AN OUTDOOR POOL, A MARBLE TILE BATH LIES WAITING WITH ITS OWN REFRESHMENT. THE BATHROOM RESPECTFULLY AVOIDS FLASHY COLORS AND BUSY WHITE-GROUTED GRIDS, CHOOSING INSTEAD A SMOOTH POLISHED MARBLE SO AS NOT TO DETRACT FROM THE SITE'S PEACEFUL MOUNTAIN VISTA. IN ADDITION TO COVERING THE FLOOR AND TUB SURFACES, THE MARBLE EXTENDS UP THE CORNER PILLAR THAT LIES BETWEEN THE TWO GLASS BLOCK WALLS.

Opposite: RESTING ON TWO TILED PILLARS, AN ARCHED TRELLIS FORMS A LEAFY BOWER AT ONE END OF THIS INDOOR POOL. THE TILES' DEEP AQUA COLOR IS A FAVORITE CHOICE FOR POOL DESIGN, APPRECIATED FOR THE LOVELY HUE IT IMPARTS TO THE WATER. TO PROMOTE SAFETY, THE SAME AQUA TILES RUN ACROSS THE EDGES OF THE POOL STEPS, MAKING THE TRANSITION FROM ONE LEVEL TO THE NEXT EASIER TO SEE.

Right: POOLSIDE FURNITURE NEEDS TO BE PRACTICAL, WATER-RESISTANT, AND ATTRACTIVE. THIS WOODEN STORAGE TRUNK, USED TO STORE SNORKELS, DEFLATED RAFTS, AND THE POOL VOLLEYBALL NET, HELPS KEEP THE POOL AREA NEAT BETWEEN SWIMS. THE TILES RUNNING ACROSS THE TOP SURFACE ARE A BONUS, ENABLING THE TRUNK TO BE USED ALTERNATELY AS A POOLSIDE COFFEE TABLE, A CATCHALL FOR WET TOWELS, OR SEATING FOR AN OVERFLOW CROWD.

◧ PART THREE ◧
PAINTING TEXTURED WALLS

INTRODUCTION

If you're reading this at home, take a look around you. Are your walls interesting? Texturally inviting? More than one color? We have become so accustomed to plain white or neutral walls that it's quite easy to overlook other choices—especially for the home. While white will always be considered classic, walls with texture and color can transport our rooms beyond the limitations of the plain white box.

All of the wall finishes pictured in this section were achieved with paints, glazes, washes, and painting tools such as rags, sea sponges, combs, and brushes. Some of these finishes are the work of skilled artists, but some were done by novices, regular homeowners brave enough to experiment with these unconventional approaches.

Many of the finishes shown here involve layering and removing color to create mottled or aged-looking surfaces. For any skill level, these approaches can be exceptionally forgiving; there is no right or wrong result, just general principles on how to proceed. Ragging and sponging, for example, employ somewhat vigorous

Opposite: THIS ROOM HAS BEEN GIVEN A DECIDEDLY COUNTRY FLAVOR THROUGH PAINT. THE WALLS HAVE BEEN RAGGED IN A SCHEME THAT IS DARKER ON THE BOTTOM AND BECOMES LIGHTER AS IT MOVES UP THE WALL. A CHEERY BORDER PATTERN IS STENCILED WHERE THE WALL MEETS THE CEILING. A TROMPE L'OEIL BIRD PERCHED ON A STENCILED VINE PEEKS UP AT A HAND-PAINTED FLITTING BUTTERFLY. **Above:** A TROMPE L'OEIL DEPICTION OF A CLASSICAL LANDSCAPE IMBUES THIS ORDINARY LIVING ROOM WITH A SENSE OF GRANDEUR.

arm and wrist motion, and the end result of these techniques will vary from one person to the next depending on the individual's touch and the tools used to achieve the effect. (For a primer on tools and techniques, see the Painting Textured Walls Appendix on page 272.)

While most home furnishings and decorations are acquired through hours of diligent scouting, shopping, and schlepping, painted finishes take shape right in the home. This on-site development has distinct advantages. You can easily fine-tune a color to the perfect shade to serve as a backdrop for your couch or carpet, and you'll have the opportunity to evaluate the overall effect under natural and artificial light at your leisure in the best possible setting—your own home. Compared to other expenditures, the cost of painting tex- tured walls is reasonable; and if you're not happy with the end result, all you'll have invested in is a few gal- lons of paint. Considering the price of some home improvements the cost of a decorative paint treatment is quite minimal.

Opposite: THIS BEDROOM COMES ALIVE IN LIVING COLOR. A SPONGE TECHNIQUE WAS USED TO WASH THE WALLS IN A BRILLIANT YELLOW HUE THAT GIVES THE ROOM A SUNNY PERSONALITY. **Above:** IN THIS INDUSTRIAL-TYPE SPACE, THE PARTIAL WALLS THAT SERVE BOTH AS ROOM DIVIDERS AND STORAGE RECEPTACLES FOR BOOKS AND COLLECTIBLES HAVE BEEN PAINTED IN A MARBLELIKE FASHION.

The layering techniques involved in these treatments make it easy to cover a "mistake" without starting over; you can lighten a color that's too dark, warm up a cool color, and work similar alchemy simply by applying additional coats of a paint or glaze. The wall's imperfections will be similarly camouflaged, so that if a wall started out as less than smooth, no one will notice this because of the magical effect of paint.

These techniques lead naturally to the development of "color" rooms, a key principle of decor in previous centuries that has been lost until recently in this century. You may find that after living for a decade or so in a home with all-white rooms, you will actually get a psychological lift when you move among rooms of contrasting colors, moods, and personalities. No matter how saturated a room's color becomes, the intensity is always relieved by change. Each room of color in your home will serve to dramatize and set off the other rooms.

The pages that follow in this section will offer specific ideas as well as general inspiration for three types of painted walls: those that look old, time-worn, and antique in Reviving the Past; those that rely on depth and saturation of color in Living Color; and those that combine various techniques to produce artisan effects such as faux stone and marble in Home Art. Together, they will illustrate the many decorative room backdrops that can be obtained using household tools and ordinary paint products.

Opposite: A RAGGING TECHNIQUE HAS GIVEN THIS WALL AN ALMOST METALLIC APPEARANCE. ROUGH-EDGED STONE CHAIRS AND A PART MARBLE, PART CEMENT FLOOR CONTINUE THE THEME SET BY THE WALLS.

Reviving the Past

Taking comfort in the past can be a great pleasure. Old furniture, textiles, pictures, and books have a humbling influence on us, serving as cultural reminders that our contemporary perspective is but one way of looking at the world. Those who truly cultivate their love of old things throw the impulse to update and modernize into reverse, striving instead to make the new look old, and the old look older.

Using freshly applied paints and glazes is an affordable way to give a home the personality, character, and lineage of time-worn surfaces. Nondescript walls, floors, and furniture can be believably transformed into faux stone, sunbaked adobe, marble, and other textures that have historical, cultural, or regional associations. The resulting

decor is satisfying to live with, as it approaches the room in its entirety instead of focusing on the furnishings alone.

The "new" old finish is practical in yet another way as well. A real stone wall is cold and damp, real marble loses its polished sheen over time, and century-old plaster eventually chips and disintegrates into powdery dust. The faux antique finish, in contrast, requires practically no upkeep and, with the application of a proper sealer coat, can even be washable.

This section features a variety of distressed surfaces that were actually created in recent times with contemporary paint products. Each surface achieves a sense of age and permanence that enhances the decor.

Opposite: Aristocratic homes and furnishings that show signs of benign neglect convey an aura of romanticism. Here, one or two layers of a lightly tinted green glaze allow a hint of natural wood grain to show through, suggesting a paint finish that has been wearing away slowly for a century or two. **Above:** A plaster wall, with its intrinsically rough surface, made a convincing canvas for a faux stone façade. To suggest venerable age, contrasting highlights were applied at random with a rag and deliberately kept simple, subtle, and few in number. The opening of the beehive fireplace, in contrast, was surrounded by a broad band of slate blue paint in order to magnify its unusual shape.

Right: A SPATTERED PAINT FINISH ABOVE THE CHAIR RAIL AND WARM YELLOW TONES BELOW IT SPARK SOME LIFE INTO A GRAND ROOM GONE TO SEED. THE SMALL FORTUNE NEEDED TO RESTORE SUCH A HOME OFTEN COMES IN FITS AND SPURTS, MAKING A QUICK YET INSPIRING INTERMEDIARY DECOR A NECESSARY OPTION BUT PROVIDING THE CHANCE TO TEST FUTURE COLOR COMBINATIONS IN THEIR ACTUAL SETTING. **Below:** PLANNING A ROOM AROUND TWO COLORS OFTEN HELPS A JUMBLE OF POSSESSIONS TO APPEAR MORE INTERRELATED. THE DEEP VIOLET AND ORANGE COLORS CHOSEN FOR THIS TWO-TONE DISTRESSED WALL JOIN RANKS WITH A BLUE TABLECLOTH, RUSSET LEATHER BOOK SPINES, AND NATURAL WOOD FRAMES. A PASSION FOR ANTIQUITY IS UNDERSCORED BY THE PRESENCE OF TWO SCULPTED MARBLE BUSTS.

Opposite: THE PLAIN CEMENT FLOOR OF THIS ENTRY HALL GAINED INSTANT PATINA WHEN TERRAZZO STRIPES WERE PAINTED ON ITS SURFACE. THE GLAZE BEARS REALISTIC SCRATCHES AND SCUFFS, A CLEER ARTIFICE SUGGESTING THE FOOT TRAFFIC OF A BUSY NINE-TEENTH-CENTURY HOTEL LOBBY. PLACING THE FLOOR STRIPES AND A MARBLE-TOPPED TABLE ON THE DIAG-ONAL HELPED TO CORDON OFF TWO CORNER DOORS THAT ARE NO LONGER IN USE.

Above: A GENTLY RAGGED WALL MAKES A RESTFUL, UNDERSTATED BACK-DROP FOR ANTIQUE FIXTURES, SUCH AS THIS THREE-ARMED BRASS SCONCE. THE DULL PATINA OF THE BRASS WOULD LOOK DIRTY AND UNPOLISHED AGAINST A CRISP WHITE WALL, BUT HERE IT GLOWS SOFTLY AGAINST A SALMON GLAZE'S HAND-RUBBED BLUSH. NOTE HOW THE DARK RED AND BROWN GLAZES EMPHASIZE THE VERTICAL MOLDING AT THE LEFT. **Opposite:** THE SOARING CEILING THAT INFUSES A HOME WITH PRECIOUS LIGHT AND VOLUME RARELY OFFERS PERSONALITY AS WELL. TO RESCUE THIS CONTEMPORARY LIVING ROOM FROM ALL-WHITE STERILITY, THE FIREPLACE WALL WAS WASHED WITH A DULL, BRICK RED GLAZE AND THEN DISTRESSED USING A VARIETY OF TECHNIQUES. THE FINISHED WALL STANDS LIKE AN ANCIENT RUIN IN THE MIDDLE OF THE ROOM, AS IF THE REST OF THE HOUSE HAD BEEN BUILT AROUND IT.

Below: TO DRAW OUT THE WARM GLOW FROM THE HEARTH INTO THE ROOM, THE WALLS, FIREPLACE, AND CEILING OF AN ADOBE-STYLE HOME ARE ALL TREATED WITH THE SAME APRICOT WASH. THE SUBTLE COLOR VARIATIONS THAT EMERGE WHEN THE WASH IS APPLIED HELP SOFTEN AND CAMOUFLAGE IRREGU-LARITIES IN THE PLASTER SURFACE. THE FINISHED SURFACE CREATES A MAGICAL BACKDROP FOR DANCING EVENING SHADOWS.

Below: PAINT IS OFTEN USED INSTEAD OF STAIN TO CAMOUFLAGE DIFFERENT TYPES OF WOOD THAT APPEAR IN THE SAME PIECE OF FURNITURE OR CONSTRUCTION. IN THIS UPPER-STORY ALCOVE, THE LOOK OF AN ARCHITECTURAL BUILT-IN WAS ACHIEVED WITH STOCK MOLDINGS, ORDINARY DRYWALL, AND A SIMPLE UNFINISHED WOOD DESK. TO UNIFY THE VARIOUS ELEMENTS, A SUCCESSION OF GLAZES RANGING FROM EMERALD GREEN TO DEEP TURQUOISE WAS BRUSHED ON EACH SURFACE AND THEN RAGGED OFF. THE MUTED, GENTLY STRIATED PATINA THAT RESULTED LOOKS DECADES OLD.

Above: WHEN A COLLECTION OF TAILORED FURNISHINGS STARTS LOOKING TOO RIGID AND PREMEDITATED, A SOFTLY TEXTURED WALL MAY BE ALL THAT'S NECESSARY TO TONE DOWN THE HARD EDGES. EVERYTHING IN THIS ROOM EXHIBITED CRISP, GEOMETRIC LINES, FROM THE MARBLE-TOPPED BUREAU WITH GOLD-BANDED DRAWERS TO THE SLEEK, SATIN-COVERED CHESTERFIELD CHAIR. THE RAGGED WALL INTRODUCES AN UNIMPOSING FEMININE PRESENCE THAT SHOWS OFF ALL THE PIECES TO ADVANTAGE.

Left: A FRESH COAT OF PAINT
FOLLOWED BY SELECTIVE LIGHT
SANDING TURNED A BANK OF
ORDINARY TWENTIETH-CENTURY
KITCHEN CABINETS INTO AN OVER-
SIZE COLONIAL DRESSER. AN
ANTIQUE WITH ORIGINAL PAINT
THAT MIGHT FLAKE OR PEEL OFF HAS
NO PLACE IN A FOOD PREPARATION
AREA, BUT THIS DELIBERATELY DIS-
TRESSED FINISH, WHICH CAN BE
DUPLICATED ON NEW UNFINISHED
WOOD FURNITURE AS WELL, MAKES
AN IMPRESSIVE SUBSTITUTE.

Right: A CHARMING BUILT-IN BOOKCASE WAS A SELDOM USED AND BASICALLY OVERLOOKED AMENITY WHEN THE WALLS OF THIS ENTRY FOYER WERE PAINTED THE PREDICTABLE WHITE. A FRESH COLOR WASHING WITH YELLOW GLAZE BROUGHT THE FRAMED UNIT BACK INTO FOCUS AND INSPIRED A COZY CORRESPONDENCE CORNER, COMPLETE WITH A DOG BED. OTHER PIECES WERE ADDED TO COMPLEMENT THE NEW ROMANTIC MOOD, AMONG THEM THE LAND-SCAPE PAINTING PROPPED CASUALLY AT THE BACK OF THE DESK.

Below: AN EFFORT TO STRIP AWAY STUBBORN LAYERS OF PAINT LEFT BEHIND A MOTTLED SURFACE WITH LOTS OF TACTILE INTEREST. TO SOFTEN AND INTEGRATE THE REMAINING FRAGMENTS, A LIGHT, NEUTRAL GLAZE WAS WASHED OVER THE ENTIRE WALL. LIKE A BUILDING THAT HAS STOOD THE RAVAGES OF TIME, THE RESULTING FINISH IMPARTS SOLIDITY AND PERMANENCE. A CHAIR STUDDED WITH BOTTLECAPS IN A TRAMP-ART STYLE STANDS IN SHARP CONTRAST AND ADDS A CONTEMPORARY TOUCH.

Above: TO GIVE THIS OLD-FASHIONED UTILITARIAN BATHROOM AN AIR OF LUXURY, THE REMODELING BUDGET WAS SUNK INTO A CUSTOM-MADE PINK MARBLE TUB SUR-ROUND. THE WALLS WERE RAGGED IN A DELIBERATELY SUBDUED GRAY TO AVOID OVERPOWERING THE MARBLE'S DELICATE PINK VEINING. A SALVAGED OVERMANTEL WITH A MIRROR MOUNTED ABOVE THE TUB ADDS A QUIRKY TOUCH AND PREVENTS THE ALL-WHITE FIXTURES FROM APPEARING TOO CLINICAL.

Above: A BEDROOM IN A SUBTROPICAL CLIMATE FEELS A FEW DEGREES COOLER WHEN THE WALLS ARE PAINTED TO RESEMBLE LARGE BLOCKS OF GRAY STONE. THE GENTLY MOTTLED SURFACE IS NEUTRAL AND UNOBTRUSIVE, UNDERSCORING THE ROOM'S SERENE MONOTONE FURNISHINGS AND CLASSIC WHITE LOUVERED SHUTTERS. ADJUSTING THE MOVABLE SHUTTERS TO DEFLECT THE LIGHT ALSO HELPS TO COOL THE ROOM.

Left: A FEW HAIRLINE
CRACKS WANDERING ACROSS
THE SURFACE OF A PLASTER WALL
MAKE A SYMPATHETIC ACCENT
TO A PIECE OF ANTIQUE NEEDLE-
WORK MOUNTED FOR DISPLAY.
THE GOLDEN ECRU COLOR
WASHING MATCHES THE
NEEDLEWORK'S YELLOWED
FABRIC, BRINGING THE EXQUISITE
GREEN EMBROIDERY INTO RELIEF.
ADDITIONAL GREEN TONES
APPEAR IN THE TRIO OF
PILLOWS GROUPED ON THE
SETTEE BELOW.

LIVING COLOR

The power of color in interior design can not be underestimated, for color is perhaps the most basic and pervasive influence a decor can impose. Chosen wisely, the colors in a home will cheer, uplift, and invigorate the occupants as well as relax, soothe, and pamper them.

Color is never static. Its mood changes throughout the day, responding to passing rays of sunshine, heavy clouds, and glowing lamps. The intensity and natural beauty of any hue is greatly enhanced when glazes are used to build color on a wall or floor surface. Color is, after all, reflected light. When there are more layers to reflect, the color is enriched without necessarily turning darker or losing its initial sparkle. Adding those multiple layers requires patience, but the results are worth the effort.

The photographs in this section capture the variety of color moods that glazes can bestow upon an interior. Some of the rooms have muted watercolor hues that are soft and cloudlike, while others exhibit strong tactile properties. Each setting is a trailblazer, opening up new color territory on the home frontier.

Above: ORNATE ARCHITECTURAL MOLDINGS IN VICTORIAN HOMES WERE TRADITIONALLY GILDED AND PAINTED IN SEVERAL COLORS TO HIGHLIGHT THE DETAILS. UNFORTUNATELY, CENTURY-OLD WOOD, GESSO, AND PLASTER MOLDINGS ARE PRONE TO CHIPS AND DENTS, AND SHRINKAGE CAN CAUSE ENTIRE SECTIONS TO BREAK OFF. HERE, A DEEP GREEN COMBED GLAZE BRINGS OUT ALL THE BEAUTY OF AN OLD DECORATIVE MOLDING WHILE CAMOUFLAGING ITS IMPERFECTIONS.

Opposite: A LUSH GOLDEN WASH SPILLS FROM THE CEILING ONTO THE WALLS OF A DINING ROOM, SUGGESTING A LUXURIOUS PRIVATE CHAMBER IN A MARBLE PALACE. THE CREATION OF ENCLOSED, ELEGANT INTERIORS IS AN ART PRACTICED BY RESTAURATEURS WHO WANT TO PROVIDE THEIR PATRONS WITH A BRIEF ESCAPE INTO ANOTHER WORLD. THE SAME SENSE OF PRIVACY, SECURITY, AND PAMPERING IS ALWAYS WELCOME AT HOME.

Below: TO GIVE AN OVAL MAHOGANY PARTNER'S DESK A CONTEMPORARY AIR, ITS COMPLEMENT, A DEEP TEAL BLUE, WAS CHOSEN FOR THE WALL FINISH. THE SOFTLY RAGGED WALL HAS A CLOUDLIKE QUALITY THAT OFFERS AN ESPECIALLY RESTFUL VISTA AFTER A PERIOD OF CONCENTRATED READING OR PAPERWORK. THE BLUE LAMPSHADE REINFORCES THE SERENE SCHEME, WHILE LEAFY PALM FRONDS ADD LUSHNESS TO THE VIEW.

Above: A TIGHT FLOOR PLAN ALLOTTED ONLY THE BARE MINIMUM OF SPACE AT THE FOOT OF THIS L-SHAPED STAIRCASE. TO HELP REGULATE THE TRAFFIC FLOW, A SIDE WALL WAS GLAZED A SUNNY YELLOW, AND A RECTANGULAR, KNOTTED RUG WAS LAID ON THE FLOOR. THOSE DESCENDING THE STAIRCASE HAVE AN EASY GLIMPSE OF BOTH THE WALL AND THE RUG, ALLOWING THEM TO NAVIGATE THE PASSAGE WITH GREATER EASE.

Left: YELLOW WALLS WOULD HAVE APPEARED TOO PLAYFUL AND UNSOPHISTICATED FOR THIS ESSENTIALLY SPARTAN INTERIOR, HENCE THE SOLUTION TO GO HALF AND HALF. THE YELLOW DADO ADDS SUNNY COLOR WITHOUT OVERWHELMING THE SPACE WITH FRIVOLITY, WHILE THE WHITE WALL ABOVE MAKES A FITTING BACKDROP FOR A TRADITIONAL RELIGIOUS PRINT. THE OVERALL RESULT IS CONTEMPORARY AND ELEGANT IN ITS SIMPLICITY.

Right: BOTH NATURAL AND ARTIFICIAL LIGHT SPREAD THEIR INDIVIDUAL AURAS ACROSS THIS BEDROOM WALL, DEMONSTRATING THE RANGE OF INTENSITY AND TONE THAT A SINGLE PAINT COLOR CAN HOLD. IN BRIGHT DAYLIGHT THIS CORAL WASH APPEARS PALE, BUT IN EVENING BY LAMPLIGHT IT TAKES ON A WARM ORANGE GLOW. BOTH TONES COMPLEMENT THE BLUE STRIPED BEDSPREAD AND PAINTED BEDSTEAD, CABINET, AND CHAIR.

Below: REVERSING THE USUAL COLOR ASSIGNMENTS CAN GIVE A ROOM A MYSTERIOUS, SURREALISTIC AIR. UNLIKE TYPICAL INTERIORS, IN WHICH WALLS ARE LIGHTER THAN FLOORS, THIS DINING ROOM FEATURES A DARK MAHOGANY WASH ABOVE A PALE ECRU CARPET. WHILE VISUALLY OUT OF THE ORDINARY, THE JUXTAPOSITION IS ALSO SERENE, PERHAPS DUE TO THE ROOM'S MINIMAL STYLE AND THE WARMTH OF THE WOOD FURNITURE AND MOLDINGS.

Above: A STEPPED HALF-WALL—PART OF A LARGER CUTOUT ENTRY—CREATED A SWEEPING VISTA BETWEEN THE LIVING ROOM AND DINING ROOM IN THIS HOME, MAKING COLOR COORDINATION BETWEEN THE TWO AREAS ESSENTIAL. TO AVOID THE MONOTONY OF A SINGLE COLOR, THE DINING ROOM WALLS WERE GLAZED, THEN BRUSHED ON THE DIAGONAL TO CREATE A TEXTURED EFFECT THAT LOOKS WINDSWEPT. THE CONTIGUOUS VISTA IS HARMONIOUS, YET EACH ROOM RETAINS ITS OWN IDENTITY.

Below: IN ROOMS USED PRIMARILY FOR EVENING ENTERTAINING, RICH DARK WALLS CREATE A ROMANTIC, SEDUCTIVE AURA. THE EVOLUTION OF THIS WALL'S COLOR SCHEME—FROM APPLE GREEN TO DARK GREEN TO ULTRAMARINE TO MIDNIGHT BLUE—AROUSES MORE INTEREST THAN JET BLACK, YET IS NO LESS SOPHISTICATED. AGAINST THE WALL'S DEEP COLORS, A SEATING ARRANGEMENT IN CINNAMON AND ORANGE HUES STANDS OUT LIKE A SPARKLING JEWEL.

Above: WHEN THE ARCHITECTURAL DETAILS OF A ROOM ARE AS GRAND AS THIS, NOTHING ELSE SHOULD STEAL CENTER STAGE. TO HELP THE WALLS RECEDE INTO THE BACKGROUND, A DEEP PEACOCK BLUE GLAZE THAT MATCHES THE CHAIR UPHOLSTERY WAS WASHED OVER THEM. GOLD-TONED MARBLEIZING ON A WHITE GROUND, IN TURN, FOCUSES ATTENTION ON THE FLUTED PILASTERS, DEEP BASEBOARD, AND DECORATIVE CORNICE MOLDING. AN AUSTRIAN SHADE ECHOES THE DAPPLED COLORS AND FREESTYLE MOTION OF THE VEINING.

Left: A WASH THAT INTENSIFIES THE CLOSER IT GETS TO THE CEILING IMITATES NATURE'S SKY, WHICH ALWAYS APPEARS LIGHTER AND LESS SATURATED NEAR THE HORIZON. FRAMING THE IMAGINARY VISTA ARE DECORATIVELY PAINTED LEAFY ARCHES, WHICH, ALONG WITH THE MINI-ÉTAGERÈ AND UNIQUELY SHAPED LIGHT FIXTURE, IMBUE THIS SMALL, RATHER UTILITARIAN BATH-ROOM WITH OLD WORLD ELEGANCE.

Left: TO MAKE A WIDE ENTRANCE AND SWEEPING SQUARE FOOTAGE APPEAR EVEN MORE SPACIOUS, THE WALLS WERE COLORED WITH SKY BLUE GLAZE. THE COOL COLOR VISUALLY RECEDES, MAKING THE FAR WALL APPEAR FARTHER BACK THAN IT ACTUALLY IS. DARK BROWN DIAMONDS STENCILED ONTO THE FLOOR SUGGEST A DISTANT VANISHING POINT AND PROVIDE A STRONG CONTRAST TO THE SKY EFFECT. DESPITE THE PREPONDERANCE OF BLUE ON THE WALLS AND FURNISHINGS, A SMALL ADDITION OF WHITE WOODWORK, RED THROW PILLOWS, AND ECLECTIC WALL SCONCES DRESSED WITH BLACK STARS KEEPS THE MOOD VIBRANT AND UPBEAT.

Above: PLACING "EARTH" COLORS BELOW AND "SKY" COLORS ABOVE PROVED TO BE A SUCCESSFUL FORMULA FOR PAINTING A MAIN-FLOOR ENTRY FOYER. EACH SURFACE—TERRA-COTTA WALLS AND THE LIGHT BLUE CEILING—IS FRAMED BY PRISTINE WHITE WOODWORK TO DISTINGUISH IT FROM THE OTHER.

Above: DRAWING ATTENTION AWAY FROM A HIGH CEILING IS ESSENTIAL TO CREATING INTIMACY IN A CAVERNOUS BEDROOM. ON THE FAR WALL, A CHALKY BLUE GLAZE LENDS A HAND BY EXTENDING NO FARTHER THAN THE STANDARD HEIGHT OF CEILINGS IN NEWLY BUILT HOMES. A LINE-UP OF SMALL FRAMED PHOTOS ON THE MANTEL AND A BUST ON THE HEARTH ALSO HELP DRAW INTEREST DOWNWARD, AWAY FROM THE FORMAL ANCESTRAL PORTRAIT LOOMING ABOVE.

Below: TO GIVE THE INTRINSIC BEAUTY OF FREE-FORM AND SYMMETRICAL PATTERNS AN OPPORTUNITY TO STAND OUT, TRY PLACING THEM SIDE BY SIDE. THIS GLAZED WALL WAS DRAGGED WITH A COMB FROM VARIOUS DIRECTIONS, CREATING RANDOM CONTOURS SIMILAR TO THOSE SEEN IN AERIAL PHOTOGRAPHS OF CULTIVATED FIELDS. THE SYMMETRICAL PATTERNS ON THE ADJACENT DRAPERY PANEL APPEAR ALL THE MORE PRECISE IN CONTRAST. THE SECRET TO THE JUXTAPOSITION'S SUCCESS IS THAT THE TWO WALLS ARE SIMILAR IN TONE.

Left: THIS UNUSUAL ARCHITEC-
TURAL SPACE FEATURED SO MANY
INTERESTING ANGLES, LEDGES, AND
BUILT-INS THAT THERE WAS NO
OBVIOUS FOCAL POINT. TO PRO-
VIDE SOME CONTRAST, A DEEP
CORNFLOWER BLUE GLAZE WAS
WASHED ACROSS THE FIREPLACE
WALL. INSPIRED BY THE TERRAZZO
KITCHEN FLOOR IN THE FORE-
GROUND, THE BLUE GLAZE
COMPLEMENTS AND THUS SETS OFF
THE GOLDEN-TONED WOOD
FURNITURE AND FLOOR.

Right: STANDARD BOOKCASE UNITS CAN PROVIDE WELCOME STORAGE, BUT IF THEY DON'T FIT THE WALL SPACE, THEY CAN LOOK GANGLY AND HAVE NO REAL AFFILIATION WITH THE ROOM. TO CONSOLIDATE THESE MATCHING UNITS ALONG ONE WALL, FLUTED PILASTERS WERE PLACED BETWEEN THEM. STOCK MOLDING CLOSED THE GAP BETWEEN THE SHELVES AND THE CEILING, AND ALSO DOUBLED AS PEDIMENTS. TO ENSURE THAT THE PILASTERS STOOD OUT, THE SURROUNDING WALLS, CEILING, AND TRIM WERE GLAZED AND RAGGED IN SOFT GREEN AND DUSTY PINK TONES THAT PROVIDE UNITY AND COLOR YET FADE SOFTLY INTO THE BACKGROUND.

Above: A SENSE OF INTIMACY WAS HARD TO CREATE IN THIS HIGH-CEILINGED ROOM, PARTLY BECAUSE THE TOWERING WINDOWS KEPT DIVERTING ATTENTION UP FROM THE SEATING AREA. TO EMPHASIZE THE LOWER HALF OF THE ROOM, AN ORANGE-RED DADO WAS RAGGED ALL AROUND. A LARGE RED BOLSTER CLEVERLY EXTENDS THIS LINE STRAIGHT ACROSS THE WINDOW SEAT, WHILE THE OTHER FURNISHINGS WERE DELIBERATELY SELECTED TO FALL BELOW THE NEW CHAIR LINE. ABOVE IT, THE RAGGING TEXTURE CONTINUES TO CREATE WARMTH BUT IN HUES THAT ARE LESS INTENSE, THUS PROVIDING A SENSE OF SPACE.

Opposite: RED IS THE STEREOTYPICAL COLOR CHOICE FOR BISTROS AND FAMILY RESTAURANTS, FOR IT IS KNOWN TO STIMULATE THE APPETITE AND AROUSE THE TASTE BUDS. IN THIS DINING ROOM, ALMOST EVERYTHING IS COLORED RED, FROM THE RAGGED WALLS AND MASSIVE CORNER CUPBOARD TO THE PATTERNED TABLECLOTH. THE SATURATION ENABLES THE FEW REMAINING PIECES TO STAND OUT IN STARTLING CONTRAST. NOTE HOW THE WHITE CEILING PROVIDES VISUAL RELIEF FROM ALL THE EXCITEMENT WITHOUT TAKING AWAY FROM THE DRAMA. **Below:** IN A FORMAL HOME, THE VESTIBULE CONVEYS THE TONE AND STYLE OF THE OVERALL DECOR. THIS GENEROUS ENTRYWAY WELCOMES VISITORS WITH WARMTH AND A SENSE OF ORDER, YET THE APRICOT COLOR-WASHED WALLS HINT THAT THERE MIGHT BE SOME FUN SURPRISES IN THE ROOMS BEYOND.

Above: DISPLAYED AGAINST A WHITE WALL, A BEAUTIFUL COLLECTION OF BLUE-AND-WHITE CHINAWARE PLATTERS SIMPLY FADED INTO THE BACKGROUND. TO PROVIDE MORE CONTRAST AND SHOW OFF THE SHAPES OF THE PLATTERS BETTER, THE WALL WAS WASHED WITH A PALE TANGERINE GLAZE, ANOTHER EXAMPLE OF HOW OPPOSITES ON THE COLOR WHEEL CAN CREATE STRONG VISUAL INTEREST.

Above: PAINT THAT SIMULATES EXPENSIVE STONE MAKES FOR A RICH JUXTAPOSITION OF COLORS AND TEXTURES. IN THIS POSTMODERN TABLEAU, A BRILLIANT TURQUOISE SURFACE, RAGGED TO IMITATE MALACHITE ORE, SHARPENS THE STEELY EDGE OF THE INDUSTRIAL SHELVING. THE WALL AND SHELVING WORK TOGETHER TO SHOW OFF THE VULNERABLE BEAUTY OF TWO LONG-STEMMED TULIPS IN A CRYSTAL BUD VASE.

Left: STRIPED FABRIC AND A BOLDLY COMBED WALL SURFACE ARE NATURAL COMPANIONS, NO MATTER WHAT THE DECOR. IN THIS FORMAL SETTING, ROMANTIC BALLOON SHADES SEWN FROM YELLOW TONE-ON-TONE STRIPED FABRIC MIMIC THE SOFT VERTICAL STRIATIONS ON THE ADJACENT WALL. MORE STRIPES APPEAR ON THE GOLD-EDGED LAMP SHADE. FOR THE BEST OVERALL ENSEMBLE, THE VARIOUS GROUPS OF STRIPES SHOULD BE OF DIFFERENT WIDTHS AND DIFFERENT BUT HARMONIOUS SHADES OF COLOR, RATHER THAN EXACT MATCHES.

Opposite: THREE TIERS OF COLOR ARE A FINE WAY TO BREAK UP THE MONOTONY—OR THE INTENSITY—OF A SINGLE-COLOR ROOM. THIS DESIGN PLACES A HEATHERY FIELD AT EYE LEVEL, A SUNNY YELLOW BAND AROUND THE UPPER PERIMETER, AND A TROPICAL TURQUOISE SKY OVERHEAD. THE BLUE OF THE CEILING WORKS TO OPEN WHAT MIGHT OTHERWISE BE A CRAMPED SPACE, AND THE TRANSITION FROM HEATHER TO YELLOW CREATES THE SAME HORIZONTAL LINE AS AN OLD-FASHIONED PICTURE-HANGING MOLDING. THE PALE AQUA DOTS ADDED TO THE MAUVE SURFACE PREVENT THE CEILING FROM APPEARING ALOOF.

Above: SMALL ROOMS ARE THE PERFECT CANVASES FOR TRYING OUT BOLD DECORATIVE STROKES THAT CAN BE OVERPOWERING ELSEWHERE. IN THIS BATHROOM, BLACK PAINT APPLIED TO THE WALL WITH THE EDGE OF A SPONGE MIMICS EXPERIMENTAL ACID ETCHING. A SEAMLESS MIRROR EXTENDS THE IMAGE LIKE A RORSCHACH INKBLOT, BLURRING IT EVER SO SLIGHTLY IN A WATERY HAZE. THE ENTIRE SCHEME IS FUTURISTIC YET HAS AN ART DECO FEELING, THANKS TO ITS CHROME FIXTURES AND SLEEK BLACK SURFACES.

Opposite: WITH WINDOWS ON THREE SIDES, THIS ENCLOSED PORCH MADE SLEEPING HERE ALMOST LIKE CAMPING UNDER THE STARS. TO ENHANCE THE ROOM'S OUTDOORS FEELING, AN OLIVE GREEN WASH WAS LAVISHED ON THE SIDE WALL, AND TURQUOISE PAINT WAS APPLIED TO THE TOP AND BOTTOM OF THE WINDOW FRAMES TO OPEN THE ROOM TO THE SKY. THE STRIPED HUDSON BAY BLANKET ON THE BED TURNS THE ALCOVE INTO A BONA FIDE BUNKHOUSE.

Above: ABUNDANT NATURAL LIGHT STREAMS THROUGH A GLAZED DOOR AND A SKYLIGHT—THOUGHTFUL AMENITIES FOR A DARK INTERIOR VESTIBULE AND STAIRWELL. TO FURTHER BLUR THE DISTINCTION BETWEEN OUTDOORS AND IN, THE WALLS WERE WASHED WITH A PEACH GLAZE AND CRAZED WITH A RAG TO RESEMBLE SUNBAKED ADOBE. THE STAIRWELL IS FRAMED WITH WIDE, ROUGH BOARDS THAT ARE USUALLY RESERVED FOR EXTERIORS AND OUTBUILDINGS.

Right: TAKING ITS COLOR CUES FROM NATURE, A BUILT-IN BREAKFAST NOOK PLACES A DARKER OCEAN BLUE CLOSER TO GROUND LEVEL AND A LIGHTER SKY BLUE ABOVE IT. A MUSTARD GOLD CHAIR RAIL FILLS IN AS A SUNNY HORIZON LINE ACCENTED BY WITTY PUNCTUATION MARKS. THE LIGHT BLUE WALL PALES CONSIDERABLY IN THE LAMPLIGHT, BUT THE WASH IS ACTUALLY QUITE EVENLY APPLIED. THE SOOTHING COLORS PROVIDE A TRANQUIL BACKDROP FOR THE ECLECTIC MASK AND HUBCAP COLLECTION.

Above: BRIGHT, LIVELY PAINTS CHEER UP ONE END OF A NARROW EFFICIENCY KITCHEN THAT COULD EASILY FEEL CLAUS-TROPHOBIC. THE BANANA-COLORED WALLS LOOK SUNNY EVEN ON OVERCAST DAYS, AND TURQUOISE PAINT MAKES TWINS OUT OF TWO MISMATCHED CHAIRS. THE RED-TOPPED CABINET DOUBLES AS A TABLE FOR QUICK MEALS AND SNACKS.

Above: SELECTING ACCESSORIES FIRST IS A SENSIBLE APPROACH TO DECORATING CLASSIC BLACK AND WHITE-TILED BATHROOMS, WHICH LOOK FABULOUS NO MATTER WHAT COLORS ARE USED AS ACCENTS. THIS WALL PALETTE IS A SOPHISTI-CATED TAKE ON THE MULTICOLOR-CHECKED SHOWER CURTAIN. THE CLASSIC WATER JUG PRINT INSPIRED THE MARBLED EFFECT, CREATED HERE BY SPONGE-WIPING. KEEPING ALL THE COLORS THE SAME TONE ENSURED THAT THE FINISH WOULD BE SUBTLE, DESPITE THE RANGE OF COLORS USED.

Home Art

Many homes are overly dependent on white walls, those silent partners that show off paintings, sculptures, and collected objects with museum-like objectivity. While stunning in a public space, the "gallery" look offers a private home little warmth or uniqueness.

A colorful, decorative wall finish will move the focus of color and texture onto the walls, endowing a room with personality and presence. The space itself will become a cherished treasure.

Any ordinary flat wall can figure more prominently in the decor through faux landscapes and marbled

walls. Some of the wall treatments here fully transform the space by adding new vistas or dimensions, while others contribute in more modest ways. By coordinating existing furnishings with the finishes—or sometimes eliminating the furniture altogether—daring new rooms are created for not much more cost than that of the paints.

Classic or offbeat, playful or somber, decorative finishes show a generous spirit. Single-handedly, they can inspire even the most mundane interiors to come alive.

Above: Everything in this comfortably furnished bedroom revolves around a deep mahogany hue, which surfaces in the carpet, dressing table, textured wall, and bedspread. The magnificent serpentine spines on the dressing table give the room a quirky charm, with their unique, surreal presence cleverly underplayed by the matching wall treatment, a compromise solution for roommates with divergent tastes.

Opposite: Stones from imaginary quarries bestow their colorful faux finishes on the walls and ceiling of this small vestibule, giving it a luxurious prominence. The novel application of various colors—mauve, apricot, green, and rose—plays delightfully against the crimson and blue columns, and is bound to intrigue and delight the senses longer than a solid color.

Below: CORINTHIAN COLUMNS FLANKING A TEMPLELIKE DISPLAY NICHE APPEAR ALL THE MORE DRAMATIC WHEN THE ADJACENT WALLS ARE PAINTED TO RESEMBLE STONE. THE DEPTH OF THE NICHE GIVES THE IMPRESSION THAT THE STONE IS SEVERAL FEET THICK, PROMOTING A SENSE OF SOLIDITY AND SANCTUARY. THE ONLY GIVEAWAY IS THE PAINTED SWITCH PLATE NEAR THE MOLDING AT THE LEFT.

Above: WALLS THAT ARE PLAIN ARCHITECTURALLY NEEDN'T LACK GEOMETRIC INTEREST. EACH ZIGZAGGING BAND ON THIS DINING ROOM WALL IS GLAZED IN A DIFFERENT COLOR, ACCENTUATING THE MOMENTUM OF THE DESIGN. USING TINTS AND SHADES OF THE CHOSEN PALETTE ENSURES THAT NO COLOR IS REPEATED YET HELPS ALL THE COLORS REMAIN INTERRELATED. THE SUEDELIKE TEXTURE WAS ACHIEVED BY RAGGING OFF THE WET GLAZE WITH A WAD OF CHEESECLOTH.

Left: GENEROUSLY SIZED DOORS THAT OPEN ONTO A PASS-THROUGH FROM THE KITCHEN MADE THIS DINING AREA CEILING SEEM DISPROPORTIONATELY HIGH. TO FORESHORTEN THE WALLS, A CHAIR RAIL WAS ADDED AROUND THE ROOM, DIVIDING THE WALL INTO TWO SECTIONS. THE DADO WAS COLORED WITH A DARK RUSSET GLAZE SO THAT IT WOULD APPEAR AS AN EXTENSION OF THE FLOOR, WHILE THE REMAINING WALL ABOVE WAS PAINTED IN A LIGHTER TONE AND THUS READS AS THE "REAL" WALL. EACH SECTION IS TEXTURED WITH THE BASE COAT COLOR OF THE OTHER, A CLEVER WAY TO DRAW THE TWO SECTIONS TOGETHER.

Right: WHEN A ROOM'S NATURAL VISTA IS LESS THAN ATTRACTIVE, A GIFTED HAND CAN PAINT A SCENE TO SUIT ONE'S FANCY. THIS BEAUTIFULLY RENDERED LANDSCAPE TURNS AN ORDINARY DINING ROOM INTO A BALCONY OVERLOOKING TUSCANY'S HILLS. CONTINUING THE SKY ON THE CEILING FOSTERS THE ILLUSION OF ENDLESS OPEN AIR, WHILE THE COLUMNS AT THE FRONT OF THE PICTURE PLANE UNIFY THE MURAL AND THE ARCHITECTURE OF THE ROOM.

Below: HERE, AN UNUSUAL PAINT FINISH SPILLS FROM THE WALL ONTO THE FLOOR. A MONOTONE TEXTURE CAN APPEAR ESPECIALLY SURREAL IN A WINDOWLESS ENTRY OR HALLWAY WHEN THERE IS LITTLE IN THE WAY OF FURNITURE OR OTHER VISUAL CLUES TO COMMUNICATE WHICH END IS UP; IN THIS CASE, A TAPERED-LEG CONSOLE TABLE LENDS A HELPING HAND.

Above: UNFORTUNATELY, THE GAPING BLACK HOLE OF A HEATING VENT WAS ON PERMANENT DISPLAY IN THIS OTHERWISE LIGHT AND AIRY FOYER. TO DRAW ATTENTION AWAY FROM THE VENT, A TEXTURED PAINTING TECHNIQUE RESEMBLING TIGER'S MAPLE WAS WORKED ON THE LOWER WALL, WHILE THE GRATING WAS PAINTED WHITE TO HELP KEEP THE EYE FOCUSED ON THE TRIANGULAR GRILLWORK RATHER THAN THE BLACKNESS LOOMING BEYOND IT. A CONSOLE TABLE PLACED ABOVE THE VENT HELPS TO CONCEAL IT FROM THE CASUAL VIEWER, TOO.

Above: ENVISIONING A NICHE AND STATUE WHERE NEITHER EXISTS IS A FIRST STEP TOWARD TRANSFORMING A FLAT WALL INTO ONE WITH PICTORIAL DEPTH. A PROFESSIONAL ARTIST USED VARIOUS RAGGING, WASHING, AND BRUSHWORK TECHNIQUES TO PRODUCE THE TROMPE L'OEIL EFFECT SHOWN HERE. FAR FROM PLAYING SECOND FIDDLE TO THE REAL THING, A RENDERING SUCH AS THIS POSSESSES A LIFE AND SPIRIT ALL ITS OWN.

Below: A COLLAGE OF ARCHITECTURAL PRINTS, DECOUPAGED DIRECTLY ONTO THE WALL, CALLED FOR A UNIQUE UNDERLYING BACKGROUND. THE APT SOLUTION WAS A RAGGED SURFACE THAT RESEMBLES PARCHMENT. THE PRINTS WERE AFFIXED TO THE SURFACE, AND TROMPE L'OEIL RINGS, CORDS, TASSELS, AND FRAMES WERE ADDED LAST, COMPLETING THE ARTFUL DECEPTION.

Left: MARBLEIZING ALL FOUR WALLS WOULD HAVE OVER-WHELMED THIS COMPACT DINING ROOM, SO JUST ONE SURFACE WAS DECORATED. THE PAINTS USED FOR THE MUSTARD WALLS AND OLIVE-GLAZED BOOKCASES WERE REPEATED IN THE MARBLE VEINING FOR A HIGHLY COORDINATED LOOK. SLIGHTLY DARKER SHADES IN THE VEINING ECHO THE BRONZE MIRROR FRAME ABOVE THE CHAIR.

Opposite: THE FIXTURES OF THIS COMPACT POWDER ROOM WERE AWK-WARDLY PLACED, GIVING PRIME FLOOR SPACE TO AN INACCESSIBLE CORNER. TO MINIMIZE THE FLAW, A PLEASANT MURAL DRAWS THE EYE UP AND OUT BEYOND A TROMPE L'OEIL TRELLIS TO A CLOUD-FILLED SKY. THE BAS RELIEF, TRELLIS, STONE HALF-WALL, AND BIRDS ARE ALL HAND-PAINTED ON THE WALL SURFACE WITH PERCEPTIVE DETAIL.

Below: WHEN PAINTED DETAILS PLAY A SUPPORTING ROLE TO OTHER FUR-NISHINGS, A CONVINCING STAGE SET CAN EMERGE. HERE, A PAST-ITS-PRIME COUCH WAS DRAPED WITH A RED THROW AND KILIM RUGS, TURNING A DULL CORNER INTO A VIBRANT MIDEASTERN BAZAAR. LENDING CREDENCE TO THE TRANSFORMATION IS THE WALL'S LOW DADO, PAINTED WITH A SERIES OF MOORISH-INSPIRED OGEES.

Above: A BUILT-IN BANK OF CUPBOARDS AND DRAWERS PROVIDED MUCH-NEEDED STORAGE FOR AUDIO AND VIDEO EQUIPMENT, BUT THE WOOD'S LIGHT TONES PROVED TOO INFORMAL FOR THE ROOM'S DECOR. A CONSERVATIVE DARK GREEN GLAZE HELPED THE CABINETS GAIN A LITTLE MAJESTY AND RECEDE GRACEFULLY INTO THE BACKGROUND. THE INDIVIDUAL PANELS ON THE CABINET DOORS WERE RAGGED TO SHOW OFF THE MOLDINGS THAT SURROUND THEM.

Below: IN A ROOM USED MAINLY AT NIGHT, DARK, MYSTERIOUS COLORS ARE APPROPRIATELY SEDUCTIVE. THE SWIRLING TORTOISESHELL PATTERN ON THE WALL WAS CREATED WITH RAGS AND BRUSHES, OFFERING A LABYRINTH OF VISUAL DELIGHT NO MATTER WHEN IT IS VIEWED. THE INTEREST INTENSIFIES AT NIGHT, WHEN THE DARK COLORS SEEM TO ENVELOP AND PROTECT THE ROOM. DEEP RED DRAPES THAT DRAW SHUT COMPLETE THE ENCLOSURE.

Above: AN ALLOVER RAGGED TEXTURE IN A LIGHT COLOR ENHANCES, RATHER THAN INTERRUPTS, THE STRONG, SOLID LINES OF A GABLED CEILING. THE MOTTLED ECRU TEXTURE RESEMBLES PARCHMENT, A FITTING CHOICE FOR THIS MASCULINE RETREAT WITH CONTINENTAL FURNISHINGS. A PRINTED WALLPAPER BORDER EDGES THE SKYLIGHT ABOVE ADDS A FEELING OF SPACE.

Left: When accessories are bold and strong-boned, a background that extends rather than saps their energy is a must. Here, wavy combing creates an invigorating backdrop for a Venetian mirrored sconce, a moody landscape in a silver frame, and an Italian side chair: all three pieces have sinuous curves that are echoed in the combing. The effect is dynamic, even though the glaze is a subdued taupe.

Right: A SECTION-BY-SECTION ANALYSIS REVEALS THE SECRET OF A FIREPLACE MANTEL'S CHARM: IT IS ACTUALLY A GLORIOUS ASSEMBLAGE OF STOCK LUMBERYARD MOLDINGS. EACH PIECE IS METICULOUSLY HAND-PAINTED TO RESEMBLE QUARRIED STONE IN REAL AND FANCIFUL COLORS. THE QUIRKY LOOK IS AMPLIFIED BY THE OCHER PAINT CHOSEN FOR THE WALL.

Below: HERE IS A VASE OF FLOWERS THAT NEVER NEEDS REPLACING. THIS VESTIBULE WAS TOO NARROW FOR A CONSOLE THAT COULD HOLD A VASE OF REAL FLOWERS, SO THE WALL WAS UPDATED WITH A TROMPE L'OEIL VASE IN ITS OWN ROMANESQUE NICHE. ARCHITECTURAL MOLDINGS AND A BROKEN PEDIMENT ABOVE THE DOORWAY INSPIRED THE CLASSICAL THEME.

Above: IN AN ATTIC ROOM, A COMBINATION OF HORIZONTAL AND VERTICAL LINES HELPS TO MINIMIZE THE WALL'S STRONG UPWARD SLOPE. BOTH ARCHITECTURAL AND PAINTED DETAILS APPEAR IN THIS CLASSICAL, SYMMETRICAL DECOR, AND EACH IS SO PERFECTLY EXECUTED THAT ONLY CLOSE INSPECTION CAN DISTINGUISH THE FAUX FROM THE REAL. THE SUNNY YELLOW AND WHITE PALETTE IS PARTICULARLY SUITED TO A SETTING WHERE DORMERED WINDOWS COMPROMISE INCOMING LIGHT.

Above: WHEN STRONG GEOMETRIC LINES DOMINATE A ROOM'S LANDSCAPE, PLAYFUL COLORS CAN HELP LIGHTEN THE ATMOSPHERE AND MAKE ARCHITECTURAL DETAILS APPEAR LESS RIGID. IN THIS BEDROOM, AQUA, YELLOW, AND GOLD GLAZES COLOR THE PANELS, MOLDING, DOORS, AND WALL SO THAT THEY APPEAR LESS SERIOUS AND IMPOSING. UPON COMPLETION OF THE PROJECT, THE ALL-WHITE CEILING LOOKED CONSPICUOUSLY BARE, SO IT WAS WASHED WITH AN AQUA GLAZE AND GIVEN ITS OWN MOCK PANEL, TOO. NOTE HOW EMPHASIZING THE RECTANGULAR AND SQUARE SHAPES POINTS UP THE MARBLEIZED FOOT OF THE BED.

Below: ANY SURFACE IN THE HOUSE IS FAIR GAME FOR PAINTED DESIGN. THIS RUG DESIGN MAKES SENSE UNDER THE WINDOW, WHERE IT CAN BE APPRECIATED, INSTEAD OF ON THE UNSEALED FLOOR, WHERE IT WOULD HAVE BEEN WORN AWAY BY FOOT TRAFFIC. NOTE HOW THE PAINT COLORS PICK UP THE YELLOW CEILING AND RED DOOR.

Left: ACCOMPLISHED AND BUD-
DING ARTISTS ALIKE CAN APPRECIATE
THE INFORMAL CANVAS A PAIR OF
OLD KITCHEN CABINET DOORS PRO-
VIDES. IF A PAINTING EFFORT
DOESN'T PAN OUT, THE DOORS
CAN ALWAYS BE PAINTED OVER OR
REPLACED. THIS ABSTRACT HARLE-
QUIN DESIGN, RENDERED IN
MIRROR IMAGE, WAS A DEFINITE
ARTISTIC SUCCESS.

PART FOUR

DECORATING WITH ARCHITECTURAL DETAILS

INTRODUCTION

Architectural details provide new ways to think about decorating. When most folks hear the word "decorating," they immediately think of painting and papering, or changing the furniture and drapes. But adding architectural details is an attractive alternative because it is a more piecemeal approach—something you can do a piece at a time without interrupting your life too much or spending exorbitant amounts of money. By introducing trim here, changing a countertop there, or incorporating offbeat objects into a decor, you can animate your living space and give it your own distinct stamp.

One way of introducing details into the home is to turn to manufacturers and retailers who fabricate and sell new moldings, trim, and fixtures. From reproduction plaster rosettes to tony brass spigots, a variety of embellishments can be acquired by approaching these sources. But a more exciting—and often more economic—alternative is presented by the world of architectural salvage. Here you will find trimmings that are one of a kind—embellishments that

Opposite: THIS CLASSICAL TRANSITION FROM COOKING TO DINING AREA IS EFFECTED LARGELY BY TWO HALF-COLUMNS. THE SPACE'S OPEN DESIGN ALLOWS THE EYE TO ROAM FREELY BETWEEN THE TWO ROOMS BEFORE THE BODY ACTUALLY TRAVERSES THE STATELY PASSAGE. NATURAL WOOD, BOOKS, AND A FESTIVE FLOOR KEEP THE TONE LIVELY. **Above:** NEOCLASSICAL MOLDING THAT RUNS ALONG A ROOM'S EDGE WHERE THE WALL AND CEILING MEET ADDS A TOUCH OF ELEGANCE TO AN OTHERWISE ORDINARY ROOM. WHIMSICAL PAINTED STARS ABOVE AND BELOW CALL ATTENTION TO THIS BEAUTIFULLY CARVED ARCHITECTURAL EMBELLISHMENT, WHILE REVEALING A SENSE OF HUMOR ON THE PART OF THE HOME'S OWNERS.

are as unique as their makers. With architectural salvage, you embark upon an adventure, discovering beautiful and unique details that will add character to your home.

Everyone loves a bargain and the thrill of finding something valuable that has previously gone unnoticed. When you do stumble across that special treasure, you have not only keen eyes and great insight to thank, but good luck—the gift of the gods. There is definitely something alluring and a little magical about finding architectural salvage. Why, for example, does fragile stained glass survive the wrecker's ball when sturdy materials such as concrete and stone are often reduced to rubble? And how is it that shortly after you decided to redo the den, you just happened upon the perfect mantel in a garage up the street?

There is something a little exotic about the pieces themselves, too, as if they have been protected by Fate. Some of the rarer and more expensive materials come from Europe—from grand houses in England, Italy, or France. For these pieces to have traveled such a great distance, somebody clearly smelled a gem in the rough— or a nice profit. But as is often the case, your great find may have traveled from just across town, where one more highway interrupted the slumber of a stately old Victorian home. Many other pieces of salvage survive by whimsy alone, and each one is sure to have its own individual story.

But why is decorating with architectural artifacts such a hot practice? There are a variety of different answers, depending on who you talk to. Love of a bargain is one possibility. On a more pragmatic level, though, architectural remnants are wonderful for filling holes in the decor that want...something. (You'll know it when you find it.) Hunting for salvage is also a revitalizing antidote to the weekday blahs, drawing you to explore old shops on Saturday morning while most people are still rubbing sleep out of their eyes. Some people purchase salvaged objects as investments to resell later. And others just need something to do with their hands—to fill time and garages.

Larger social forces may be at work, too. People are spending a lot more time at home these days, and while they are not exactly staring at the walls, they are noticing things that might have been overlooked during the go-go eighties. People like their abodes to be appealing retreats, where they can forget their cares and—when possessed with a bit more energy—share who they are with their guests.

The growing trend toward conservation and a lack of tolerance for mindless consumption also come into play. If something is worthwhile, why not save it? Part of that attitude has to do with growing up, of course, for as we mature we seek not only comfort but meaning; a big part of salvage's appeal is that it has a context, some historical significance. It came from someplace; it was part of somebody's life; and now it is part of yours. And like you, it has a story to tell.

Which brings us to the real appeal of salvage: it offers a chance to tell your story, to express yourself. In a time of relentless change, you can build a place where you can be yourself, regardless of what the crazy world outside is doing. And along the way, you will learn a lot.

For one thing, your eye will acquire a great education. Like bird-watching or learning French, the more you practice, the more proficient you become. You will notice architectural details everywhere you go, and you will be able to distinguish great finds from also-rans. Go shopping for ornamental brackets, for example, and on the way home you will find yourself scrutinizing every house on the block for similar details. The more you learn, the richer your world becomes.

Your imagination will also prosper from these outings. Once you have figured out how to obtain more light in that spare bedroom (with some stained glass, perhaps?), you will start ruminating about replacing that tacky kitchen linoleum with fieldstone. It's contagious. You will be surprised at how adept you can become at solving problems; in fact, those troublesome elements of the decor cease to be problems and become a source of fun. Then, when you really get into salvage, you will start looking for trouble, buying oddball objects that go with nothing yet somehow make it all work. The rules go out the window. Sandstone slabs as tabletops? Corrugated tin roofing on the bathroom walls? Why not? Go ahead—spread your wings.

Above: Wonderful found fragments, no two alike, chase each other across a wall to form a one-of-a-kind frieze. Offering a refreshing visual distraction, this unique embellishment is an inventive alternative to ordinary trim.

GLASS

We humans are born loving light—perhaps because we are built that way. Our eyes can see in starlight or sunlight, distinguish seven million different shades of color, change light into nerve signals, and, every second, send a billion pieces of fresh information to our brains.

Is it any wonder, then, that glassmaking is among the most ancient of arts? Glass is a wondrous material: it can change the color of sunlight and permit our eyes to look through walls. And the right window in the right place can certainly change our moods. Hence, glass—stained, leaded, or plain—is an essential tool of any designer.

Once you have found that special piece of glass, get to know it. Hang it over an existing window and observe its colors at different times of day. Put swatches of fabric next to it and think about the interaction of colors and shapes.

Does it suggest an architectural style that is harmonious or contrasting? (Conflicting styles can impart great energy to a home's "active" rooms.) A great window can spawn a whole new look for a decor. And do not forget the more mundane virtues of glass: adding even a small window or a mirror makes a tiny room look bigger; stained glass along a stairway saves electricity and improves safety; and translucent or textured glass admits light to more personal areas, such as bathrooms, without sacrificing privacy.

One of the great boons of searching for that perfect piece of glass is that the quest sharpens the eye, inspiring you to look more closely at everything. You will find yourself walking along streets that you thought you knew, seeing colorful, exquisite architectural details for the first time. Oh, brave new world that has such windows in it!

Opposite: Stained glass is great for setting or fine-tuning a mood. Here, a small recycled piece of stained glass with touches of deep red helps evoke a lush late-Victorian feel, yet at the same time provides a little visual relief from it. Although most everything here is rich in hue, from the cabinets to the trim to the heavy curtains, the elegant floral motif of the stained glass is an airy counterpoint to a dining room that might otherwise be a tad too formal. **Above:** A painted glass beauty such as this, with prismatic jewels around the border, can be put to a multitude of uses. Because it is so heavily figured, this vibrant piece is ideal for transforming a window that currently does not have much of a view. Or the glass could be illuminated from behind and hung on a wall as a piece of glowing art.

Below: SETTING A RESTFUL TONE, SHADES OF BLUE SOFTEN THE UPPER WINDOWS OF THIS ENCLOSED PORCH AND CREATE THE ILLUSION OF AN INDOOR SKY. MEANWHILE, THE WINDOWS THAT ARE CLOSER TO EYE LEVEL REMAIN FREE OF COLOR AND DETAILING SO AS TO PROVIDE A CLEAR VIEW OF THE OUTDOORS. THE BLUE-AND-WHITE COLOR SCHEME OF THE PORCH'S ARCHITECTURAL ELEMENTS IS ECHOED BY THE CHINA PROUDLY DISPLAYED ON DELICATE GLASS SHELVES.

Opposite: ESCHEWING THE TRADITIONAL HEADBOARD, THIS BED IS PLACED UP AGAINST A WALL FEATURING SYMMETRICAL STAINED GLASS WINDOWS THAT BRING WELCOME LIGHT AND COLOR TO THE ROOM. THE YELLOW AND BLUE HUES OF THE GLASS CONTRIBUTE TO THE SPACE'S COUNTRY TONE, WHICH IS FURTHER ENHANCED BY AN AIRY OAK LATTICE INGENIOUSLY MOUNTED ABOVE THE BEDROOM ENTRANCE. THE LATTICE ALSO PREVENTS THE OUTER AREA FROM APPEARING TOO BLAND WHEN THE WHITE POCKET DOORS ARE CLOSED.

Above: THIS TOWERING WALL EXPANSE IS ENLIVENED WITH THE HELP OF A DIAMOND-SHAPED STAINED GLASS WINDOW BEARING AN EXQUISITE ABSTRACT DESIGN. THE SURROUNDING WOODEN BEAMS CREATE AN OFFBEAT—AND SLIGHTLY OFF-CENTER—FRAME THAT CALLS ATTENTION TO THE GLASS ARTWORK BEYOND, LENDING IT AN AIR OF IMPORTANCE.

Opposite: LIKE SPICES OR SCENT, THE RIGHT PIECE OF GLASS CAN GO A LONG WAY. THIS KITCHEN DINING AREA IS DEFTLY ENHANCED BY LEADED WINDOWS FROM THE LATE NINETEENTH CENTURY. WITH THEIR MINIMALIST DISPLAY OF COLOR, THESE WINDOWS MAINTAIN THE ROOM'S SENSE OF SIMPLICITY AND ALLOW THE DECOR'S RICH WOODWORK TO SHINE THROUGH.

Above left: THIS CURVED WINDOW AND ITS GRACEFUL SIDELIGHTS DRAW THE EYE OUT INTO THE WORLD. HAD THE WINDOW'S TRIM BEEN PAINTED WHITE, IT WOULD BE FAR LESS EMPHATIC; BUT STRIPPED AND STAINED AS IT IS, THE WOODWORK BECOMES THE PERFECT FRAME FOR AN IMMENSE AND CONSTANTLY CHANGING CANVAS. TOGETHER, THE ARCHING GLASS AND ENCOMPASSING TRIM LEND THE SPARE LOFT A CLASSICAL FEEL AND MAKE AN OTHERWISE GRAY CITYSCAPE LOOK LIKE A MOMENT CAPTURED IN TIME. **Above right:** STAINED GLASS WINDOWS PROVIDE A WONDERFUL OPPORTUNITY FOR SETTING A THEME. DECKED WITH PEPPERS, SQUASH, CORN, GRAPES, AND A COLORFUL FISH, THESE CHEERY WINDOWS BRIGHTEN UP AN EARTH-TONED KITCHEN. TO PREVENT THESE LIVELY PIECES OF GLASS FROM BEING DWARFED BY THE SURROUNDING STONEWORK, THE CARPENTER BUILT UP THE WOOD CASINGS AROUND THE WINDOWS.

Above: WHEN ILLUMINATED, SHADES OF HONEY AND AMBER PROVIDE A WARM, NATURAL GLOW THAT BLENDS IN BEAUTIFULLY WITH THE SOFT LUSTER OF WOOD. THIS SOOTHING OVERHEAD LAMP WAS CREATED BY THE GREENE BROTHERS, TURN-OF-THE-CENTURY DESIGNERS WHOSE AESTHETIC EVOLVED OUT OF THE ARTS AND CRAFTS MOVEMENT. **Opposite:** THIS GREENE BROTHERS FIXTURE FILTERS SOFT LIGHT THROUGH ITS GOLDEN TINTED GLASS, CREATING A PEACEFUL AMBIENCE FOR A RELAXING DINNER. SHINING DIRECTLY ABOVE THE DINING TABLE, THE LIGHT IS GENTLY REFLECTED BY THE HIGHLY POLISHED MAHOGANY.

Right: THIS DETACHED BATH-HOUSE IN THE RAIN FOREST OF OREGON IS ONE OF THE MOST SERENE PLACES ON EARTH—ESPECIALLY LATE IN THE DAY WHEN RARE RAYS OF WINTER SUN FILTER THROUGH THE FIR TREES. A FIRE BURNING IN THE WOODSTOVE, A STEAMING BATH IN THE COMFORTABLE OLD CLAW-FOOT TUB, AND A FANCIFUL STAINED GLASS SCENE COMBINE TO CREATE THE PERFECT SPOT FOR PEACE AND REFLECTION. THE WORLD BECOMES A MYSTICAL, MAGICAL PLACE WHEN SEEN THROUGH THIS CONTEMPORARY GLASS CREATION DESIGNED BY TENOLD PETERSON. THIS IS LIVING AS IT SHOULD BE: UNWORRIED AND UNHURRIED.

Above: WHAT CAN BE DONE WITH ONLY A SMALL SECTION OF SALVAGED GLASS? SCULPTOR TENOLD PETERSON SET THE FACETED JEWELS OF AN OLD WINDOW INTO THIS LUMINOUS LEADED GLASS SHADE HE FASHIONED FROM SCRATCH. WHEN STAINED GLASS WINDOWS ARE OUT OF THE QUESTION, A LAMP SUCH AS THIS IS A WONDERFUL WAY OF GRACING A ROOM WITH THE COMBINED BEAUTY OF COLOR AND GLASS.

Above: RUSTIC YET SOPHISTICATED, OPEN YET COZY, THIS BATH IS A STUDY IN CONTRASTS. THE ETCHED-GLASS BULRUSHES BEHIND THE TUB ECHO THE NATURAL WOOD OF THE ROOF TRUSSES AND THE PLANTS REPOSING AROUND THE ROOM. MEANWHILE, THE FLOOR, COUNTER, AND TUB SURROUND HAVE A MORE POLISHED FLAVOR WITH THEIR GRANITE-COLORED WATERPROOF TILE. THE GREAT UNIFIER IS THE SUNLIGHT, WHICH MAKES ITS GRAND ENTRANCE THROUGH AN EXPANSIVE SKYLIGHT, CAUSING THE BRASS TO GLEAM, THE WALLS TO GLOW, AND THE BODY TO REJOICE.

Below: GLASS BLOCKS, POPULAR IN THE 1950S, ARE MAKING A BIG COME-BACK—AND FOR GOOD REASON. THEY ARE PRACTICAL AS WELL AS ATTRACTIVE, AND THEIR TRANSLUCENCE MAKES THEM PARTICULARLY WELL SUITED TO URBAN BATHROOMS WHERE LIGHT, SPACE, AND PRIVACY ARE AT A PREMIUM. ADDING A FLAIR OF FESTIVITY, GLASS BLOCKS CAN PICK UP COLOR FROM TOWELS AND OTHER TRAPPINGS, AS WELL AS BOUNCE BACK LIGHT FROM NEARBY FIXTURES. MORTAR JOINTS BETWEEN THE BLOCKS ADD A BIT OF VISUAL RHYTHM—A WEL-COME RESPITE FROM THE MONOTONY OF SLIDING-GLASS BATH ENCLOSURES.

Above: BEAUTY MEETS PRACTICALITY: THE CLEAR GLASS ABOVE ADMITS SUN FREELY, WHILE THE OPACITY OF THE LOWER PANELS IS PERFECT FOR PRIVACY. PLUS, THE CASEMENT WINDOW CAN BE OPENED TO VENT MOISTURE AFTER A SHOWER.

Opposite: AN ARCHED WINDOW, ITS POINT SOARING UP TO THE SKY, OPENS UP AN ALCOVE, BRINGING LIGHT AND SPACIOUSNESS TO WHAT MIGHT OTHERWISE BE A SHADOWY NOOK. THE SIMPLE PANELING ON EITHER SIDE OF THE WINDOW BLENDS SEAMLESSLY INTO THE REST OF THE ALCOVE, BUT THESE SIDES ARE ACTUALLY SHUTTERS THAT CAN BE CLOSED WHEN PRIVACY IS DESIRED. COLUMNS HIGHLIGHT THE ARCH, THEIR SIMPLE DESIGN PROVIDING THE AREA WITH AN UNDERSTATED ELEGANCE. TOGETHER, THE COLUMNS AND ARCH CREATE THE PERFECT FRAME FOR A MAGNIFICENT ANTIQUE COPPER TUB THAT IS NESTLED WITHIN THE ALCOVE. **Above:** DESPITE ALL THE WARM, LUSTROUS TOUCHES IN THIS FAMILY ROOM, THE UNIQUE PANELED DOOR MAKES A TREMENDOUS IMPACT. WOODEN PANELS HAVE BEEN REPLACED WITH TRANSLUCENT GLASS TO CREATE A PLAYFUL YET ELEGANT LOOK. MOREOVER, THIS CLEVER DOOR TREATMENT ALLOWS LIGHT TO FLOW FROM ONE ROOM TO THE NEXT.

Left: GLASS CAN BRING A FRESH LOOK TO EXTERIOR DOORS. THE INTENSE DETAILING ON THESE GLASS INSETS PREVENTS OUTSIDERS FROM HAVING A CLEAR VIEW OF THE INTERIOR AND INTRODUCES A TOUCH OF REFINEMENT TO THE RUSTIC FAÇADE. **(left top)** WITH SUNLIGHT STREAMING IN FROM BEHIND, THESE SAME STUNNING WINDOWS **(left bottom)** CAN BE ENJOYED FROM THE INTERIOR AS THEY SHOW OFF THEIR VIBRANT DESIGNS, CREATING AN UPLIFTING SENSE OF VITALITY. **Opposite:** A DAZZLING DISPLAY OF COLOR AND LIGHT IS CREATED BY THE EXTENSIVE USE OF STAINED GLASS IN THIS HIGHLY ORNATE ROOM THAT HOUSES A DINING AREA, A RELAXED SITTING AREA, AND AN INTIMATE WORK SPACE. WITH ITS GOLDEN HUES AND RADIATING WOODEN BEAMS, THE DYNAMIC STAINED GLASS ARCH AT THE FAR END OF THE ROOM APPEARS AS A GIANT SUN. A FEW SQUARES OF PLAIN GLASS HAVE BEEN INCORPORATED INTO THE CENTER OF THE ARCH TO PERMIT A CLEAR PEEK OUTSIDE. TO FURTHER GIVE THE EYES A REST, PLAIN GLASS IS USED FOR THE FULL-LENGTH WINDOWS OVERLOOKING THE GARDEN, ALLOWING THE SOOTHING GREENERY TO BE ENJOYED FROM WITHIN. TYING IN WITH THE GARDEN THEME, SHADES OF GREEN AND BLUE ARE PREVALENT IN THE STAINED GLASS THAT COVERS THE CEILING. THESE SAME HUES ARE DEFTLY ECHOED IN THE TABLE SETTING BELOW.

Wood

Wood possesses many beautiful, life-affirming qualities. In its often intricate grain, you can see the route that water once traveled, up from the earth and out through the leaves to the heavens. And though the many lovely colors of wood can be explained by various chemical properties, describing wood's rich glow invariably begs analogies to life itself.

Wood is frequently rich in history. On a hand-hewn beam, you might see the primitive adze marks made by a pioneer who was building a house out of a virgin forest. Or perhaps that ornate casing came from a dusty colonial town in Mexico, from an estate carved out by conquistadors. Suddenly, you feel your place in the continuum of time.

Visually, wood enriches any decor. It is the perfect antidote to vast expanses of Sheetrock or plaster. Carved or heavily figured, wood imparts playfulness and joy; stripped or left in its natural form, it lends a warm, rustic charm; polished so that its highlights shine, it can be formal and elegant; and painted, it can take on a relaxed provincial tone.

Wherever wood appears, it works its magic. Wood trim can tie together the disparate elements of a room, make a nondescript corner special, smooth the transition from one surface to the next, hide unsightly seams, frame a favorite window, or just repose quietly until the next time you notice how beautiful it is. In short, wood has personality.

Opposite: STRIKING RESULTS WERE ACHIEVED IN THIS KITCHEN RENOVATION BY SIMPLY ALTERNATING BANDS OF WOOD WITH WHITE WALLS AND CABINETS. THE EXPOSED BEAMS ECHO THE WIDE PINE FLOORBOARDS, AND THE ARCH AND COUNTERTOPS ARE KINDRED SOULS WITH THE BUTCHER-BLOCK ISLAND. THE FINISHING TOUCH IS THE SHINY ARRAY OF COPPER POTS AND PANS, WHICH REFLECT THE ROOM BACK ONTO ITSELF. **Above:** THIS BRACKET IS NOT PERFORMING ANY STRUCTURAL SERVICE—JUST SITTING PRETTY. ALTHOUGH BRACKETS ARE WONDERFUL FOR SUPPORTING MANTELS, WINDOW SEATS, AND BUILT-IN DESKS, THEY CAN ALSO STAND ON THEIR OWN AS INTRIGUING, EYE-CATCHING EMBELLISHMENTS.

Above: IF YOU LOVE ANTIQUES BUT WONDER HOW TO INCORPORATE THEM INTO AN ESSENTIALLY MODERN SPACE, LOOK NO FURTHER. HERE, A HAND-HEWN TIMBER WITH ITS ADZE MARKS STILL SHOWING IS SUCCESSFULLY REBORN AS A MANTEL IN A NEW HOUSE. BECAUSE THE BEAM IS SO MASSIVE AND PRIMITIVE, IT PROVIDES AN OLDER-THAN-THOU CONTEXT FOR ALL THE OTHER PIECES: THE WEATH-ERED GEESE DECOYS, THE ELEGANT CAPTAIN'S CHAIR, AND THE WIDE BOARD TABLE. A CLOCK WITHOUT HANDS IS A PERFECT METAPHOR FOR THE ROOM.

Above: ANCIENT GREECE, ANYONE? THE FLUTED WOOD COLUMNS IN THIS SEASIDE RETREAT ARE SIMPLE AND EVOCATIVE, CREATING AN OPEN, AIRY FEELING THAT IS FURTHER INDUCED BY AN IMMENSE WALL MIRROR. WITH ITS POWER OF REFLECTION, THE MIRROR INCORPORATES THE TURQUOISE SEA INTO THE DECOR AND ADDS AN INVIGORATING SPLASH OF COLOR TO THE ROOM'S NEUTRAL PALETTE.

Above: THIS ARCH WAS ORIGINALLY PAINTED, BUT BY STRIPPING AND STAINING IT TO MATCH THE OTHER WOOD ELEMENTS IN THE HOUSE, THE DESIGNER TIED THE SPACE TOGETHER VISUALLY. WITH ITS ULTRAWHITE WALLS, THE HOUSE IS EMINENTLY MODERN, BUT THE WOOD WARMS IT AND MAKES IT COMFORTABLE. LIKEWISE, THE BRICK FLOOR HELPS TO CREATE A RELAXED, LOW-MAINTENANCE DWELLING.

Above: THESE MYTHICAL GRIFFINS ARE THE SORT OF THING YOU BUY ON A WHIM AND THEN PUZZLE OVER FOR YEARS UNTIL YOU FIND JUST THE RIGHT USE FOR THEM. POSSIBILITIES INCLUDE: SERVING AS LEGS TO SUPPORT A PLATE-GLASS COFFEE TABLE; ACTING AS MATCHING POSTS FOR AN ECCENTRIC STAIRWAY; OR GUARDING THE ENTRANCE OF A MAD SCIENTIST'S LABORATORY.

Above: BECAUSE MOST BRACKETS ARE RATHER STYLIZED AND STIFF, THIS ONE IS RARE INDEED. MORE LIKE ONE OF WILLIAM BLAKE'S ANGELS THAN AN ARCHITECTURAL DETAIL, THIS SINUOUS CARVING DESERVES A SPECIAL SPOT. HERE, IT NICELY ADORNS A ROUGH PLASTER ALCOVE.

Left: A SAVVY DESIGNER RESISTED THE TEMPTATION TO CLEAN UP THIS OLD MEXICAN DOOR. CONSEQUENTLY, ITS HISTORY IS TANGIBLE TO ALL WHO ENTER. THE SPARE WHITE WALL FURTHER ACCENTUATES IT, AS IF TO SAY, "HOW MANY LIVES, CONTENT AND DESPERATE, LOVING AND GRIEVING, LIVING AND LEAVING, PASSED THROUGH THIS DOOR IN TWO CENTURIES? AND WHO WILL PASS AFTER YOU?" **Above:** SOMETIMES ARCHITECTURAL ARTIFACTS SURVIVE NOT BECAUSE THEY ARE TERRIBLY FANCY OR VALUABLE, BUT BECAUSE THEY HAVE SOME INEFFABLE SPIRIT OR CHARACTER. FASHIONED FROM MANY SHORT PIECES OF WOOD (BECAUSE LONGER BOARDS WERE DIFFICULT TO OBTAIN), THESE DOORS WERE PROBABLY COMMON WHEN NEW. BUT AS THEY HAVE WARPED AND DEEPENED IN COLOR, THEY HAVE BECOME FOLK ART. TO SHOW THEM OFF TO THEIR GREATEST POTENTIAL, A DESIGNER HAS WISELY SET THEM IN AN EXPANSE OF BUFF-COLORED ADOBE.

Above: OLD WOODEN COLUMNS ARE COMBINED WITH NEW CAPITALS, AN ARCHITECTURAL CANOPY, AND LOW MOLDINGS TO DELINEATE A MAGNIFICENT ENTRANCE. WITH THEIR PEELING PAINT, THE COLUMNS PROVIDE A POWERFUL CONTRAST TO THE SLEEK, POLISHED LOOK OF THE NEWER ARCHITECTURAL ELEMENTS, YET AT THE SAME TIME BLEND IN HARMONIOUSLY WITH THE ANTIQUE FURNISHINGS IN THE AREA BEYOND. ACCENTS OF GOLD ADD SOME SPARKLE TO THE PREDOMINANTLY WHITE SURROUNDINGS. **Opposite:** THE DESIGNER OF THIS ROOM HAD A GREAT EYE AND AN EXQUISITE SENSE OF COLOR. THE GREEN OF THE WAINSCOTING AND THE DEEP YELLOW OF THE WALLS ARE COMMONLY USED IN ARTS AND CRAFTS TILE WORK, AND THEY CONTRAST NICELY WITH THE BLUE CERAMICS AND LAMP SHADE FROM THAT ERA. RICH, DARK WOOD IS AN IMPORTANT PART OF THE PALETTE, AND THE BROWN BAND WITHIN THE CROWN MOLDING IS A DEFT TOUCH.

Above: WITH ITS DEEP REDDISH HUE, THE WOOD USED IN THIS ROOM IMPARTS A LUXURIOUS TONE TO THE OVERALL DECOR. A MULTIFACETED ORNAMENTAL COLUMN EMBELLISHED WITH DARK BANDS THAT GIVE IT ADDED DIMENSION UNITES THE CHERRY WAINSCOTING BELOW AND THE MATCHING MOLDING ABOVE, THEREBY IMBUING A SENSE OF FLUIDITY.

Above: WOODEN BALUSTERS CAN BE USED FOR ALL SORTS OF THINGS, FROM CANDLEHOLDERS TO DESK LEGS. HERE, A RENOVATOR HAS BROUGHT ADDITIONAL WARMTH AND CHARM TO A WOODBURY, CONNECTICUT, HOME BY REUSING SQUAT BALUSTERS TO CREATE A UNIQUE AND ENTICING HEARTH BENCH—GREAT FOR A FIRESIDE CHAT OVER MULLED CIDER.

Opposite: WEATHERED WOODEN PLANKING AND A RUSTIC BALUSTRADE FROM AN OLD PORCH UNITE TO FORM A NOVEL TRANSOM AND GRILLE EFFECT ABOVE THIS DOORWAY, LENDING AN AIR OF AUTHORITY TO THE BEDROOM THAT LIES BEYOND. BALUSTERS BEARING A MORE POLISHED LOOK GRACE THE WOODEN BENCH, FORMING A HANDSOME BACKREST THAT MIRRORS THE BUILT-IN SOFA FRAME OPPOSITE IT. THE VERTICALITY OF THESE ARCHITECTURAL EMBELLISHMENTS IS ECHOED BY THE POSTS OF THE HEADBOARD, VISIBLE THROUGH THE OPEN DOORWAY.

STONE

The world of stone has a lot to offer. Fieldstone, limestone, quartz, tile, marble, sandstone, brick, concrete, soapstone, granite, and cobblestone are all available for you to choose from. Although stone is generally considered to be a hard, inanimate substance, some masons swear it lives; and since most children have seen stones skipping, there may be something to the notion. Granted, none of the materials mentioned above is ever going to read the newspaper, eat spaghetti, or complain about taxes, but when properly employed, stone is remarkably warm, colorful, and—for lack of a better word—alive.

Stone is also the great mixer. Usually of a neutral or subdued color, it coordinates with almost any style, fur-

nishing, rug, or other type of trapping. Because most varieties are relatively impervious to water (porous varieties such as sandstone are not), they are often placed where there is a lot of traffic, moisture, or both. Stone is a natural for outdoor areas, and makes a handsome border for ponds and the like. But the real chemistry occurs between stone and wood: old friends in the wild, they look extraordinarily civilized when paired in your home.

Another match made in heaven is the combination of sunlight and stone. Sunlight is great for revealing all sorts of subtle hues and textures. And, as a special bonus, stone will in turn radiate the sun's warmth long after the sun itself has set.

Opposite: STONE SERVES AS A NICE BIT OF VISUAL PUNCTUATION WHERE ONE ROOM MEETS ANOTHER: HERE, THE KITCHEN BEGINS. BY FINDING A FRAGMENT OF A CORINTHIAN CAPITAL ROUGHLY THE SAME HEIGHT AS THE CABINETS, THE DESIGNER WAS ABLE TO PLACE A COUNTERTOP OVER BOTH, THEREBY EXTENDING THE WORK SURFACE AND LINKING THE DECORATIVE WITH THE PRACTICAL. Above: NOW THIS IS A TUB WHERE YOU CAN SPLASH TO YOUR HEART'S CONTENT WITH NO HARM DONE. ILLUMINATED BY DIFFUSE LIGHT THROUGH TRANSLUCENT GLASS BLOCKS, THE ROUGHLY CUT STONE SLABS COME ACROSS AS CURIOUSLY SOFT AND INVITING. THE NEUTRAL COLOR OF THE STONE ALLOWS IT TO BLEND IN SMOOTHLY WITH THE VARIOUS OTHER MATERIALS, FIXTURES, AND COLORS EMPLOYED IN THE DECOR.

Below: IF FASHION MODELS CAN BE SAID TO HAVE "GOOD BONES," SO CAN COMMODIOUS HOUSES. HERE, EXPOSED FIELDSTONE, HAND-HEWN BEAMS (WITH TRACK LIGHTING HIDDEN AMONG THEM), AND GENEROUS WINDOWS CONSPIRE TO MAKE YOU FEEL WISE AND WELCOME. ALTHOUGH PRESENTLY CASUAL, THIS ROOM COULD HOST ANY ACTIVITY—FROM A FORMAL DINNER TO A BLACK-TIE CONCERT (THE ACOUSTICS WOULD BE FANTASTIC) TO ROUGH-HOUSING WITH THE KIDS. THE POTTED TREES ARE A PLEASANT REMINDER THAT EVERYTHING IN THIS ROOM ONCE LIVED OUTSIDE. **Opposite:** THIS FIREPLACE OF RECYCLED BRICK IS WONDERFULLY FUN BECAUSE THE MASON THUMBED HIS NOSE AT THE USUAL CONVENTION OF NEATLY PLACING BRICKS IN ORDERLY HORIZONTAL ROWS. THE INSPIRING JUMBLE ADDS A LOT OF LIFE AND ENERGY TO A ROOM THAT IS OTHERWISE QUITE CONSERVATIVE.

Above: ALTHOUGH WALK-THROUGH ARCHES ARE USUALLY ELABORATE AF-FAIRS, THIS PARTICULAR ARCH QUIETLY DEFINES A WET BAR, GIVING IT A SUBTLE ELEGANCE. USING STONE OF A SIMILAR COLOR FOR THE CABINET BASE AND BACKSPLASH HELPS TIE THE AREA TOGETHER. WHEN THE SPOTLIGHTS ARE OFF AND THE BAR IS NOT IN USE, THIS CORNER OF THE ROOM RECEDES VISUALLY.

Opposite: IF THIS FIREPLACE WERE A TYPE OF MUSIC, IT WOULD BE A GRAND OPERA. YET AS SPLASHY AND DRAMATIC AS IT IS, IT TOOK A LOT OF PATIENCE AND PERSISTENCE TO COLLECT ALL THESE ELEGANT PIECES — AS WELL AS A LOT OF VISION TO USE THEM SO INGENIOUSLY. IT IS, IN FACT, A WALL OF ART: HERALDIC MEDALLIONS, GRECO-ROMAN MEN, A ROARING BEAST, AND LOVELY FLORAL FRIEZE WORK. THE FLAGSTONE HEARTH WOULD LOOK GREAT WITH A RICHLY FIGURED ORIENTAL RUG LAPPING UP AGAINST IT AND A LEATHER WINGBACK CHAIR OFF TO ONE SIDE.

Above: WE ARE SO USED TO SEEING MASONRY MATERIALS AS WEIGHTY AND FIXED THAT WE FORGET HOW FLUID, VARIABLE, AND ADAPTABLE THEY ARE BEFORE THEY HAVE HARDENED IN PLACE. IN OTHER WORDS, ANYTHING CAN BE SET INTO MASONRY, AS EVIDENCED BY THE INVENTIVE INCORPORATION OF THIS STONE FACADE INTO A BRICK MASS. AN UNEXPECTED ELEMENT SUCH AS THIS CAUSES EVERY OTHER ASPECT OF THE ROOM TO SEEM DYNAMIC, TOO, AS IF IT WERE SUBJECT TO YOUR WHIMS AND WISHES. AND, INDEED, IT IS.

Above: IN THE RIGHT HANDS, STONE, THAT MOST EARTHLY OF MATERIALS, CAN BECOME ALMOST AIRY. HERE, KAREN AND TENOLD PETERSON USED A LIGHT MORTAR TO EMPHASIZE THE SHAPES OF INDIVIDUAL FIELDSTONE PIECES, CLIMAXING IN AN ALMOST BIRDLIKE EXPLOSION OF FORMS OVER THE CENTER OF THE FIREPLACE. THE UNUSUAL-LOOKING CONTRAPTION TO THE RIGHT OF THE MANTEL IS A SALVAGED 1730s PARISIAN MECHANISM THAT, THROUGH A SERIES OF CHAINS, WEIGHTS, GEARS, AND PULLEYS, TURNS A ROTISSERIE SPIT IN THE FIREBOX.

Opposite: THE BOLD USE OF RED ARIZONA SANDSTONE MARKS THIS DINING AREA AS A PLACE WHERE SOMETHING IS GOING TO HAPPEN—GREAT CONVERSATIONS, FANTASTIC FOOD, PEOPLE YOU JUST CAN'T GET ENOUGH OF. TRUE, TABLETOPS ARE SELDOM SO MASSIVE OR IRREGULAR, BUT THEN AGAIN, SURPRISE IS A FIRST COUSIN OF DELIGHT. TOGETHER WITH THE WARM WALL COLORS, THE GAILY PAINTED COLUMNS, THE HANDSOME DARK CABINETS, AND THE UNUSUAL PEAKED DOOR IN THE CORNER, THIS STRIKING DINING SURFACE EVOKES THE FEEL OF A TUSCANY ESTATE. **Above left:** SOFT AND LUMINOUS, THIS SOAPSTONE MANTEL IS THE PERFECT CHOICE FOR A COZY BREAKFAST NOOK. THE STONE'S SMOOTH SURFACE CREATES A GENTLY SOOTHING EFFECT, AND ITS NEUTRAL HUE MAKES IT AN EASY COMPANION FOR VIRTUALLY ANY COLOR OR TEXTURE. BUT BEST OF ALL, THIS TYPE OF STONE HAS WONDERFUL HEAT-RETAINING PROPERTIES: HOURS—SOMETIMES EVEN DAYS—AFTER A FIRE HAS DIED, SOAPSTONE WILL CONTINUE TO RADIATE HEAT. **Above right:** HERE, STONE IS USED MASTERFULLY TO GIVE A SOFT, TIMELESS FEELING TO A HANDSOME KITCHEN AND TO FRAME A WINDBLOWN PINE OUTSIDE. THE KEY ELEMENTS ARE HUE AND LIGHT; THE USE OF A LIGHT-COLORED STONE AVOIDS AN OVERLY WEIGHTY OR OPPRESSIVE EFFECT, WHILE ACCENT LIGHTS BRING OUT DORMANT TEXTURES AND COLORS. THESE WARM HIGHLIGHTS WORK BEAUTIFULLY WITH THE WOODEN KITCHEN CABINETS TO CREATE AN EARTHY TONE.

Opposite: THIS RUSTIC BRICK WALL SERVES AS A POWERFUL BACKDROP FOR AN INTERESTING COLLECTION OF ODDS AND ENDS, INCLUDING A VOTIVE SHELF AND MAGAZINE RACK. IF YOURS IS AN URBAN ROW HOUSE, THERE MAY BE A SIMILARLY HANDSOME EXPANSE OF BRICK BEHIND THAT CHIPPED PLASTER OR DULL DRYWALL. FREE IT! **Above:** WHEN YOU FIND AN ARTIFACT YOU LOVE, SOMETIMES YOU NEED ONLY PUT IT OUTSIDE AND LET NATURE ACCESSORIZE IT FOR YOU. ALTHOUGH THIS TIMELESS BEAUTY ORIGINALLY GRACED AN URBAN FACADE, SHE NOW RESTS EASY ABOVE A GARDEN BENCH, WHERE SHE SERVES AS A QUIET COMPANION FOR THOSE DEEP IN THOUGHT.

Above: WITH A LITTLE IMAGINATION, YOU DO NOT NEED MUCH MONEY. ALL THE MATERIALS HERE ARE COMMONPLACE, BUT BY CREATING A STRONGLY DIAGONAL "CRAZY QUILT" OF GRANITE SQUARES, BRICK, AND MISCELLANEOUS TILE FRAGMENTS, THE DESIGNER ADDED A LOT OF VISUAL INTEREST TO A WALKWAY INTERSECTION. FLOWERS OR TREES CAN BE ADDED LATER BY PULLING UP A FEW SECTIONS OF BRICK.

Right: USING THE MATERIALS AT HAND, MOST NOTABLY SALVAGED COBBLESTONES, ARCHITECT deROY MARK CREATED AN OASIS OF CALM IN THE BACKYARD OF THIS PHILADELPHIA TOWN HOUSE. ANY DECORATIVE TOUCHES ADDED TO AN AREA SUCH AS THIS CAN BE ENJOYED TWICE—AS REFLECTIONS IN THE POND. THE WHOLE EFFECT IS DECIDEDLY FLORAL, A WELCOME COMPLEMENT TO THE SURROUNDING RECTILINEAR BUILDINGS.

A Potpourri of Salvage

Life can be a fairly predictable affair, so if you want to breathe some freshness and color into it, a good place to start is in the home. Some of the most striking decors stem from unexpected uses of salvaged objects and unusual juxtapositions, so let your imagination run wild. Have fun, and believe in magic.

Salvage can be found in a wide variety of places. Your best friend's garage, the south of France, Omaha, that flea market on the far side of town, and the warehouse district on a Sunday morning are all possible resting places for that special treasure just waiting to be discovered. Your prized find might be something as small as an antique faucet, or it may be a whole claw-foot tub; it may be as basic as a Victorian light fixture or as unusual as a rusty old soda machine.

When you do stumble upon that certain something, try negotiating the price—haggling can be fun.

Then, if you cannot decide what to do with your new acquisition, turn it upside down or sideways. If it is an outside fixture, try putting it in the bedroom or bathroom. A wrought-iron grille from a garden gate can make a beautiful headboard.

One friend makes a party of redecorating. She asks everyone to bring a potluck dish and something strange. Several potlucks later she has a mantel lined with Victorian doorknobs, several large laboratory jars filled with colorful glass shards, and a bathroom wall "papered" with vintage neckties. Although these specific adornments may not appeal to everyone's tastes, the moral of the story is "When in doubt, do the strange."

Opposite: This bathroom is particularly inviting because somebody broke a few rules. Most tubs are tucked in a corner or built against a wall, but here a magnificent claw-foot tub is the focal point of the room, beckoning those who enter to partake in a relaxing, rejuvenating bath. The painted exterior of the tub is another oddball touch that gives this charming bathroom an original flair. **Above:** If you like the shape of something, put it where you can see it. Here, two brackets—probably from the underside of a staircase—rest on a shelf behind a handsome copper-clad bathroom sink. Because they are not physically attached to the surface, they can be moved in any number of interesting configurations.

Opposite: This exquisite renovation combines two salvaged elements: an old claw-foot tub and a paneled door cut down and reused to create a tub surround. Boxing in a claw-foot in this manner solves several design problems: it provides storage space nearby, creates a finished cabinet look, does away with funky views underneath, and retains heat from the bath. Moreover, this clever arrangement gracefully hides any missing or mismatched tub feet, a common characteristic of old tubs.

Right: When combined with a masterpiece such as this, a small assortment of favorite objets d'art seems perfectly at home in a powder room. A variety of carved elements, including the capital of a column, is ingeniously used to support a lavatory. The countertop further defies convention with its unusual undulating shape.

Above left: Old plumbing fixtures are among the most prized pieces of salvage because they often predate standardization. This common but elegant tub faucet set carries with it a sense of tradition. The drooping handles and the bulbous forms are almost fluid in themselves. **Above right:** These bird and rabbit handles add a playful touch to an otherwise ordinary white porcelain sink and tile vanity. With their silver shine and intricate lines, these fixtures would be equally at home on modern and antique sinks. **Opposite:** This offbeat powder room is filled with several unusual touches that are bound to make a lasting impression on guests. Instead of being embedded within a vanity or cabinet, a salvaged porcelain washbasin is unconventionally mounted on top of an elegant marble counter, leaving the chrome plumbing fixture below exposed for all to see. This chrome element is mirrored by the vertically mounted towel racks used to support adjustable side mirrors (originally from a truck), perfect for admiring oneself from all angles. Delicate crystal chandeliers hang overhead, providing the setting with a further element of contrast.

Opposite: If you have an area dedicated to meditating or perhaps just being quiet, salvage can help define it and make it special. Here, a painted corner niche with Italian overtones joins with a highly figured wall hanging, river boulders, and a small gilt cabinet to create a serene oasis in a busy world.

Above: Fashioned from an old wooden column, this charming display stand proudly shows off a small array of decorative objects in the midst of an eclectic reading nook.

Above left: THIS WROUGHT-IRON GRILLE, WHICH AT ONE POINT PROBABLY ADORNED THE TRANSOM OF AN EXTERIOR DOOR, NOW SERVES AS A CAPTIVATING DECORATIVE BACKDROP. DESPITE ITS TREMENDOUS PHYSICAL WEIGHT, THE GRILLE SEEMS AIRY, ALMOST LACY, WHEN PAINTED WHITE. SIMILAR GRATING IS USED BENEATH THE GLASS SURFACE OF THE DINING TABLE TO PROVIDE IT WITH A LIVELY PATTERN. **Above right:** THIS ELEGANT CONSOLE TABLE WAS CREATED FROM THE TOP HALF OF AN ORNATE SALVAGED MANTEL. WITH ITS TWISTED-ROPE MOTIF, THE FORMER MANTEL BLENDS IN BEAUTIFULLY WITH THE UPPER PIECES OF THE ENSEMBLE TO EVOKE A FRENCH PROVINCIAL FEELING. **Opposite:** HALLS, HIGH CEILINGS, AND OPEN SPACES NEED NOT BE DULL. HERE, A GOTHIC ROOF FRAGMENT AND A MODERN-LOOKING ARCH JOIN IN WITH A JOYOUS JUMBLE OF PUPPETS, BRACKETS, FAUX STONE, TILE, HOPI FIGURINES, AND BOOKS TO CREATE A SPIRITED DECOR THAT EXUDES ENERGY. BY ENGULFING THE ROOM FROM FLOOR TO CEILING, THESE FASCINATING DECORATIVE OBJECTS KEEP THE EYE MOVING FROM LEVEL TO LEVEL.

Opposite: Generally, "anything goes" when using salvage. But when a house is as rich in architectural details as this Los Angeles mansion, it is important to use pieces that are appropriate. Here, an original Fortuny fixture helps to set a majestic tone in a grand foyer. Skillfully carved details give the illusion that the stately light fixture is actually being suspended by thick, opulent bands of twisted rope. **Above left:** Sometimes just turning an object ninety degrees creates a singular visual effect. Here, an etched ceiling shade is used as a sconce, affixed to a threaded post coming straight out of the wall. Gilt and recurrent diagonals on the wall behind add to the drama, creating a luminous backdrop for the still life atop the table. **Above right:** Light fixtures are all the more impressive when nearby decorative details are designed to match. Here, the swirling fluidity of this delicate Victorian light fixture (which may have started out as a gas fixture) is echoed by the lacy embossed patterns of the wall covering that lies behind it.

Above: There was a time when people moved around a lot less and thus noticed, as well as appreciated, detail in the least expected places. These turn-of-the-century brass door trimmings gladden the eye, have a pleasant heft in the hand, and pair up magnificently with dark wood. **Opposite:** Sleek elevator doors from a medical building were the perfect finishing touch for a doctor's contemporary bedroom. Highly polished, they now serve as elegantly fluted closet doors that blend in seamlessly with the silver-toned high-tech entertainment center they flank.

Above: THIS STUNNING BED IS TRULY A WORK OF ART, MASTERFULLY BRINGING TOGETHER ALL SORTS OF WONDERFUL ARCHITEC-TURAL ELEMENTS. TWO WROUGHT-IRON GRILLES THAT FORMERLY ADORNED GARDEN ENTRANCES HAVE BEEN TRANSFORMED INTO A BREATHTAKING FOOTBOARD AND HEADBOARD THAT COORDINATE BEAUTIFULLY WITH ONE ANOTHER DESPITE THEIR SEPARATE PASTS. FANCIFUL EMBELLISHMENTS GRACE THE POSTS ON EITHER SIDE OF THE HEADBOARD, WHILE DISTINCT SALVAGED FINIALS TOP OFF THOSE FLANKING THE FOOT OF THE BED.

Right: The many found objects that adorn this room, such as a weathered cabinet and two colorful painted shutters, are united only by their owner's eclectic taste and love of a bargain. A veritable work-in-progress, the decor is everchanging as new treasures move in and others are relocated. The neutral colors of the floor and trim readily embrace any and all decorative objects, regardless of their hues or textures. Moreover, these subdued tones allow the room's furnishings and accoutrements to take center stage. **Below:** This little bit of "street theater" shows how easy it is to bring the beauty of the outdoors into a home's interior. Two handsome "wave-slat" shutters screwed to the wall, a tub of geraniums, and...voilà! Your outside is in!

Below: These two recycled exterior columns create a whimsical mock-heraldic entrance to the room beyond, while bas-relief figures over the passageway complete the classical picture. If you are not lucky enough to find an old relief, a new thermoplastic mold can be affixed to the wall and painted to mimic plaster.

Above: Small touches can be delightful, especially ones that introduce new perspective to run-of-the-mill objects. This shelf, perfect for displaying a few of one's favorite things, was formerly a desk drawer. Leftover bits of paint on the bottom lend character and charm.

Opposite: Has Grandma's silver ever been in more elegant company? Someone had a lot of fun repainting the lawn chairs and dragging this old Coke machine into the dining room. And the elaborate, slightly funereal mirror behind adds to the mock formality of it all.

APPENDIX A: TILE FACTS

In use since before recorded history, tiles have traditionally been made from natural earth-dug clays, from porcelain, or from clay that has been extended with natural or synthetic fillers. The first tiles were shaped by hand or cut from thin slabs of clay, then baked in the sun or in an oven until hard. Eventually, tiles were pressed into molds by hand or machine and fired to extremely high temperatures in special ovens called kilns. To give tiles a permanent finish coat, a liquid glaze is sometimes brushed or wiped across the surface between a first and second firing. In the liquid state, glazes generally appear either gray, white, or tan, but firing these substances under high temperatures causes them to metamorphose into brilliant,

distinctive colors that chemically bond to the tile and turn hard and shiny. By painting patterns or pictures on tiles using different glaze recipes, artisans are able to produce beautiful hand-decorated tiles.

The durability of a tile and the purposes for which it is best suited depend on its composition. Vitreous tiles are hard, dense, and nonabsorbent; they are impervious to repeated freezing and thawing cycles. Glazed ceramic tiles used on bathroom floors and walls are vitreous tiles. Nonvitreous tiles are more soft-bodied, porous, prone to cracks, and sensitive to repeated freezing and thawing. Mexican terra-cotta *saltillo* tiles are nonvitreous. In addition to molded clay, ceramic, and composition tiles, today's market offers a wide variety of tiles cut from natural

stone, such as marble or slate. These dimensioned-stone tiles are installed much the same way as traditional tiles and offer an elegant upscale look for a price that is actually quite competetive, considering the tiles' longevity. Most varieties of dimensioned stone are nonvitreous, but they can be sealed, or, in the case of marble, polished to a high sheen to make them stain-resistant.

The brief descriptions that follow provide basic information about the different categories of tiles used in home decor today.

TERRA-COTTA TILES

Terra-cotta tiles are rugged and earthy in color and appearance. Made by hand or machine from natural clay, the tiles range in color from

orange-red to reddish-tan to butterscotch. Handmade versions display small irregularities in their dimensions and thickness, adding handcrafted charm to a final tile installation. Tiles cut by machine are more uniform in size and shape and are therefore easier to install in an even grid. Terra-cotta tiles provide an authentic regional touch to homes with Mediterranean and Southwestern decors.

QUARRY TILES

Quarry tiles are made of natural clays that differ from those used for terra-cotta tiles in that they can be fired to very high temperatures. Generally machine-made, quarry tiles are perfectly uniform in size and thickness. They are stronger and somewhat more vitreous tha terra-cotta tiles, and sometimes display a slight surface sheen. Quarry tiles are usually installed indoors in all areas of the home except bathrooms, where ceramic tiles offer better water resistance.

CERAMIC TILES

Ceramic tiles are strong, durable, and vitreous; they are able to withstand temperature extremes and to resist penetration by water. Made by machine to uniform sizes, ceramic tiles can be glazed to virtually any color. Shiny, smooth glaze finishes are preferred for bathroom walls, shower stalls, and kitchen backsplashes because water runs off these finishes easily without clinging. Slightly pebbly textures are better choices for floors as they help to prevent slipping. Ceramic tiles are available in a wide variety of shapes and sizes, and manufacturers typically include border, edging, and corner tiles along with square tiles so that the appropriate assemblage can be created for any custom installation.

HAND-DECORATED TILES

Hand-decorated tiles are crafted by using glazes to "paint" designs or pictures directly onto a tile. The background is traditionally white, achieved by applying a layer of liquid tin glaze over the clay or porcelain tile. Additional glazes are then applied in order to create the design, which does not appear in full color until after the tile has been fired. Popular examples of hand-decorated tiles include festive yellow, blue, and green majolica tiles from Portugal, Spain, Italy, and Mexico, and blue-and-white delft tiles from Holland.

Although the patterns on many majolica-style tiles are identical, each one bears subtle variations that are the hallmark—and the charm—of hand-painted work. Typically crafted in small family-owned shops, the tiles for fireplaces, hearths, and floor edgings can be special one-of-a-kind designs, made in limited quantity for a particular installations. Hand-painted designs are also available on some commercially made tiles, but they tend to lack the exuberant brushwork of tiles made in small batches by individual artisans.

DIMENSIONED-STONE TILES

Unlike tiles that are shaped or pressed from clay, porcelain, or combined materials and then baked in a kiln, dimensioned-stone tiles are made by extracting stone from mines and quarries and then cutting this stone to precise dimensions and thicknesses. The resulting tiles are uniform in both size and shape, and they can often be polished to a high sheen. It is sometimes recommended that a sealer be used to protect the tile if the stone is porous or likely to stain. Marble, slate, limestone, and granite are some of the stones that are availables as cut tiles. All are suitable for entry halls, living rooms, and dining areas, while polished marble and granite can be used in kitchens, bathrooms, and pool areas as well.

APPENDIX B: PAINTING TEXTURED WALLS

A fresh coat of paint has long been the easiest and most affordable way to turn a tired, drab interior into a clean, welcoming space. But even newly painted walls in exciting colors can appear flat and one-dimensional without interest or depth. Today, people who want more drama in their homes are taking their painting projects one step further, incorporating centuries-old glazing and color-washing techniques into their decorating schemes. For these techniques, the wall surface is spackled, primed, and painted with a base coat in the same manner as for an ordinary painting makeover. After the walls are properly prepared, the magic begins, as one or more coats of glaze are applied to the surface. Unlike paint, glazes are translucent. Each coat of glaze that is applied allows the layers of color underneath to filter through. The result is a rich buildup of color and texture.

Highly specialized painting and glazing techniques such as marbling and woodgraining require years of practice to master, but basic textured walls can be achieved by anyone who can wield a paint roller, brushes, sponges, rags, and paint combs. The techniques are easy to grasp and offer room for experimentation and individual expression. Since every person's touch is unique, the results will be as individual as your signature.

CHOOSING AND USING COLORS

Color is truly the heart and soul of any painted wall. There are many ways to combine colors successfully. One of the more exciting aspects of decorative painting is discovering new ways to incorporate colors into a room's overall interior design.

Most color plans start with a light or pastel base coat and then add glaze coats in darker related hues. For example, an apricot-colored base coat covered with successively darker orange- and red-tinted glazes produces a deep terra-cotta effect. The reverse combination—a lighter glaze over a dark base coat—works best if the color of the glaze is more opaque. White glaze ragged off an aqua wall several times in succession, for example, can produce a lovely summer sky look for a child's room.

Introducing a color's complement or opposite can intensify the overall palette of a wall or tone it down, depending on how the paint is applied. To give a red wall extra punch, for example, dip an old toothbrush into a green paint or glaze, and run your finger across the bristles to spatter the wall at random. The resulting tiny green dots will pop out from the red background, creating a contrast that is positively electric. But the same green glaze brushed uniformly across the red surface will have exactly the opposite effect, dulling the red tones and making them softer and more muted. You can use this muting principle to advantage if you find you have misjudged a color's liveliness or overall impact on a room and want to tone down its impact without starting over.

Another aspect to consider when creating your palette is how adjacent rooms relate to one another. Walk through the rooms, along the halls, and up and down the stairs in your home with a critical eye, noting exactly which areas can be seen from other areas. By planning your color transitions carefully, you can ensure that each room enhances rather than competes with its neighbor. For a coordinated look, try to keep the same mood—soft, understated, bold, or bright—throughout the house, even if you use different colors to express it.

To identify colors that reflect your personal vision for your home, browse through decorating books and magazines, and note when a room's ambience appeals to you. The wall color may be dominant in the decorating palette or it may act as a neutral background for upholstered furniture, window treatments, and accessories. Once you have identified a basic color that you think will work for you, explore its dimensions by mixing small amounts of glaze and testing them over a base coat painted on posterboard. By moving your posterboard sample around the room and viewing it at different times of day, you can get an idea of how daylight, lamplight, and candlelight will influence the color and enhance its subtleties.

GLAZES AND WASHES

The secret ingredient for layering on subtle texture and translucent color is glaze, a gel-like or syrupy artist's medium that can be tinted to any color and is applied over the base coat. Glaze is slightly diluted for wall painting so that you can apply it quickly and evenly in a very thin coat. Because glaze is thin and semitransparent, the layer of color underneath shows through with a soft underglow. Perhaps the most beautiful use of glazes is in Renaissance oil paintings and frescoes, where a soft blush of rose-colored glaze over the cheeks gives faces a lifelike quality.

In decorating, glaze is applied directly to a wall and manipulated while still wet to create different effects. Glaze can be dabbed off with a sponge or rag, leaving behind a textured surface, or it can be patterned by dragging a comb, brush, or other object across the glazed surface. Once the glaze has dried, a new glaze in the same or a different color can be added and the process repeated. By varying the colors and techniques, an infinite number of uniquely textured patterns can be achieved. Developing your own methods for manipulating the glaze is part of the fun.

CHOOSING A MEDIUM

The first decision to make when painting a room is whether to use oil-based or water-based paints and glazes. Each type has advantages and disadvantages, so consider the pros and cons of each carefully, since you must use the same product base throughout the project—from base coat to final glaze—for the successive layers to bind to one another properly.

Oil-based glazes are often easier for beginners to work with, as they take longer to dry, thus lessening the pressure to work quickly. The downside of oils is that they must be thinned and cleaned with flammable, often strong-smelling solvents that must be used with caution in a properly ventilated area. Some areas restrict the use and disposal of oil-based paint products to reduce their negative impact on the environment.

Water-based products are comparatively odorless, and wet paint can be washed off brushes and rollers with cool water. One way to "keep up" with faster-drying water-based glazes is to work in tandem with a partner, one person applying the glaze and the other ragging off, sponging, or combing. Special retarders designed to slow the drying time of acrylic paint products can also be of help.

OIL-BASED PAINTS

If you choose to use an oil-based system, you will need the following products:

• Eggshell or satin-finish alkyd paint
• Japan paint, artist's oils, or universal tints
• Transparent oil glaze
• Solvent (kerosene, turpentine, paint thinner)

Your base coat should be an alkyd paint with a dull eggshell or satin finish. Avoid using high-gloss or enamel finishes. Purchase enough paint for one or two base coats, following the coverage estimates on the paint can. The base coat color can be ready-mixed at the paint store, or you can custom-mix your own hue by adding japan paint, artist's oils, or universal tints to white paint. You can purchase transparent oil glaze or you can make your own by combining three parts turpentine, one part double-boiled linseed oil, and a few drops of japan dryer. Like paints, transparent oil glaze can be tinted to the color of your choice. Solvent is used to thin the glaze and for cleanup.

LATEX AND WATER-BASED PAINTS

If you choose a water-based system, you will need the following products:

• Semigloss latex interior house paint
• Artist's acrylics or universal tints
• Acrylic artist's medium

Your base coat should be a semigloss latex interior house paint. Avoid flat finishes when using latex paint; they are too dull and tend to absorb the glaze before you have a chance to rag it off. As with oils, the latex base coat color can be ready-mixed or you can mix your own color by adding artist's acrylics or universal tints. Water-based glaze is made from acrylic artist's medium, which is available in either liquid or gel form, can be diluted with water, and can be tinted different colors. Be sure to choose a medium that dries clear, not white.

PREPARING THE GLAZE

Glaze of the proper consistency glides onto walls, adheres smoothly, and, above all, does not run or drip. Unfortunately, there are no guaranteed formulas for diluting a glaze to the right consistency. Humidity, amount of sunlight, and exposure to air all affect a glaze's viscosity. When thinning an oil glaze or acrylic medium, be sure to add the solvent or water in small increments, as diluting a glaze is always much easier than trying to thicken it.

Coloring the glaze mixture also requires a light hand. To preserve the glaze's translucency, the color should be added sparingly; add just enough to tint the glaze without turning it opaque. Basic proportions for an oil-based glaze are six parts oil glaze, one part solvent, and up to one part color. Basic proportions for a water-based glaze are one part acrylic medium, three parts water, and up to one part color. The color can be taken from a single tube or can, or you can mix your own custom shade before adding it to the glaze.

When you are first learning how to mix glazes, mix a small amount in a disposable container (a sturdy paper cup will do) and jot down the proportions you used. Test the glaze on posterboard painted with a base coat and taped to a wall to make sure the color effect is what you want and that the glaze viscosity is well suited to the texturing technique you have chosen. If the glaze appears runny when you apply it or the texture you create using a rag, sponge, or comb doesn't hold up as the glaze dries, then the glaze is too thin. If the glaze is gummy and difficult to manipulate, it is too thick. When the "recipe" is right, write down the proportions so that you don't forget them, then mix a larger batch of glaze in a plastic paint bucket. Depending on the viscosity, about two quarts (1.9 l) of glaze should be enough to cover three hundred square feet (27 sq m) of wall surface. Always mix about twenty percent more glaze than your calculations indicate in order to avoid running out before you have completed your project. Even with a written recipe, achieving an exact color match can be tricky.

GETTING DOWN TO WORK

When purchasing painting equipment and tools, always buy the highest-quality products you can afford, as they will help you work more efficiently and achieve professional results. Rollers should be the spring-cage type, with ribs that support the roller pad from the inside so that it doesn't collapse. The roller pad should be thick and fluffy to hold the maximum amount of paint without dripping. Brushes should have full natural bristles securely attached to the ferrule (the cap that holds the bristles to the handle of the brush); when you spread the bristles apart, you shouldn't be able to see down to the wood. Sponges should be thick and absorbent. Don't overlook the importance of supplies such as drop cloths, buckets, latex gloves, and a brush spinner, for these materials will make your painting and cleanup time quicker and easier.

Here are a few more tips that should help you get the job done safely and easily:

- When you open a new can of paint, take a few moments to hammer nail holes one inch (2.5cm) apart around the lip, so paint that gets into the rim will drip back into the can.
- For brushwork, pour a small amount of paint into a plastic bucket so that you don't have to carry the heavy paint can up on the stepladder with you.
- Your painting wardrobe should consist of old comfortable clothes, latex gloves, and a cap with a duckbill brim.
- Open windows and keep the room well ventilated throughout the painting and drying periods.

Preparing the Wall Surface

There are two approaches to preparing a wall surface for painting. One is to make sure the walls are perfectly primed, with all holes and nicks filled in and sanded smooth. This approach ensures that the paint and glaze coats will adhere with a strong bond without cracking. Sometimes, however, longevity is not an issue. You may want to simply spruce up temporary living quarters or make a room more livable while you work out plans for a more permanent renovation. If you would like to enhance a room's "character," you can patch cracks in the plaster to prevent further damage rather than completely repair them, then incorporate the cracks into a painted finish for an eye-catching "ancient ruin" effect.

To achieve a durable, long-lasting finish, you must restore your walls to the best possible condition before you paint and glaze them. This preparation phase is time-consuming and painstaking, but the smooth surface that results is worth the extra effort. Begin by moving the furniture into the center of the room, taking down pictures, mirrors, and light fixtures, and covering everything, including the floors, with drop cloths. Fabric drop cloths are recommended because they soak up stray drops of paint and give the liquid a chance to evaporate. Avoid disposable plastic drop cloths, as spilled paint simply sits on the plastic, just waiting for you to step in it and track it all over. Unscrew and remove the switch plates and outlet covers, and tape plastic sandwich bags over all the doorknobs.

Next, examine the wall surface in indirect daylight from different angles, as this is the best way to spot cracks, dents, and other imperfections. When you find a crack or hole, dislodge any loose pieces with a scraper, then whisk away the plaster dust with a soft brush (be sure to wear a particle mask). Traces of wallpaper and its adhesive can be removed using an appropriate cleaner or a steam machine. If you find any nail heads popping up, hammer them below the surface, making a shallow dent in the drywall (nails in plaster walls, if found, should be removed). Fill in all gaps, holes, and cracks with spackling compound, using a flexible putty knife to smooth the compound over the surface as evenly as you can. When the spackle is dry, sand the surface lightly until it is perfectly smooth and even with the wall. You may have to repeat the spackling and sanding process several times, since spackle shrinks as it dries. The specific details of your wall preparation will be determined by the condition of the wall, whether it is plaster or drywall, and whether wallpaper was applied in the past.

Priming the Walls

Once the wall surface is smooth and the dust is vacuumed away, you can begin the exciting part of your project: building the layers of color. Your first layer is a prime coat. Primer is a white paint product that evens out the blotchy tones left behind by spackling, improves the coverage of the first color coat (particularly light colors), and acts as a buffer on new, bare walls so that they don't soak up the first coat of paint like a sponge. A universal primer can be used under either an oil- or a water-based base coat and also makes a good ground when you want to apply new paint over a previously painted wall. In some situations—for instance, if the new base coat is the same color and finish as the old one—you can safely omit the prime coat.

APPLYING THE BASE COAT

Once the primer has dried, you can apply the base coat. To begin, brush paint into the corners and up against the ceiling, baseboard, and trims—all the areas inaccessible to the roller. This process is known as "cutting in," and for it to be effective, the paint should be applied evenly and extend a good three inches (7.5cm) from each inaccessible edge. To properly load the brush, dip the bristles into the paint until they are halfway coated, lift the handle straight up, and then slap the bristles back and forth rapidly against the inside of the bucket to shake off excess droplets. This method lets you retain the maximum amount of paint on the inner bristles, so that you can paint smooth, even

strokes about two feet (61cm) long before reloading. With practice, you should be able to paint a straight edge against a molding or ceiling, but if you have difficulty, you can mask off these areas with low-stick painter's masking tape before you begin. If you omitted the overall prime coat, spot-prime the spackled areas with the base coat paint while the brush is still wet. Since dry spackle absorbs paint more readily than the surrounding wall surface, this step makes for more even roller coverage later on.

The fastest way to spread paint on the wall is with a roller. To wet the roller, fill the well of a roller tray or the bottom quarter of a five-gallon (19l) bucket with paint, then dip the roller into it. To shed the excess paint, roll back and forth a few times on the tray's angled plane or on a roller screen hung inside the bucket. Roll a large M shape onto the wall, then spread the paint around the wall by back-rolling in different directions. The long extension handle should let

you reach up to the ceiling and down to the baseboard without using a stepladder or having to bend over. A second coat is optional, since the glaze coats that follow will fill in and enrich the base color.

CREATING BASIC GLAZE TEXTURES

Working with a glaze on a large wall surface will be quite different from your smaller poster-board sample. To apply a glaze to a wall, work from left to right (right to left if you are left-handed) in two-foot (61cm) wide vertical sections. Start at the top of the wall and work down, first applying the glaze and then manipulating it. Move on to the next two-foot section quickly, blending the join while the glaze is still wet. This sequence ensures that the entire surface will be uniformly colored and textured. Most glaze methods involve several steps, and you should work with a partner to keep the momentum going.

To avoid smearing paint in the corners, paint opposing walls

one day, let them dry overnight, and then complete the adjacent walls the next day. Wear disposable latex gloves whenever you work with glazes, and follow the general painting guidelines regarding ventilation. Always allow plenty of drying time between applications so that you don't muddy your previous work. Specific guidelines for ragging, color washing, sponging, and dragging follow.

RAGGING

Ragging is a general term for a variety of textured painting techniques. As the name implies, the key tool is a rag, about two feet (61cm) square. Woven linen and cotton fabrics make ideal rags, but you can also achieve novel effects with cotton knits and open-weave fabrics such as cheesecloth. The edges of the rags should be cut clean with scissors, not torn, to help prevent loose threads from escaping into the paint. Cut a generous number of rags, since you will have to replace them throughout the project as they become saturated.

You can use rags to apply diluted paint and glaze to the wall, to texture glaze already on the surface, and to lift glaze off the surface. Remember, the harder you press, the more glaze you will lift off. To apply a glaze or diluted paint with a rag, saturate the rag, ring it out well, then crumple it loosely in your gloved hand and dab at the wall surface. Another method is to form the wet rag into a tube and roll it down the wall. For a less pronounced texture, apply the glaze to the wall with a brush or roller and dab at it with a crumpled rag moistened with water or turpentine to lift the glaze off. For a two-tone marble effect, brush on the glaze in random strokes that cover about half the wall surface; rag this glaze, let it dry thoroughly, then add the second color to the open spaces and rag in the same manner. You may also wish to experiment with different ragging techniques on posterboard to determine effects that please you before you begin. Regardless of which ragging style you choose, the key to an interesting overall pattern is to vary your hold on the rag continuously as you dab, so that none of the impressions repeat. To avoid smears, wait until you have lifted the rag from the surface before twisting your wrist and changing the rag's position in your hand. The texture achieved with ragging ranges from coarse to very soft, depending on how many layers of glaze you rag and the weight of your touch. Ragging does take time; consequently some people find oil-based paints more compatible with ragging techniques than faster-drying water-based paints.

COLOR WASHING

Color washing is the technique to choose when you want a soft, beautiful wall finish with the fluid quality of watercolor paints. Very thin glazes are used in color washing, making it possible to build up multiple translucent layers with cloudlike depth. The glaze is applied with a roller or brush, then smoothed lightly in all directions with a sponge or a wide brush with soft bristles that leave no brushmarks. The finished surface takes on a time-worn patina that is especially effective when a hint of the base coat shows through.

Both water- and oil-based products work for color washing, although thin water-based glazes are prone to rapid drying and may not allow you enough time to smooth and blend the glaze at the edges of each application. To slow the evaporation, sponge the wall with clear water before you apply the glaze, making sure the base coat is perfectly dry first. You can also add acrylic paint retarder to the glaze to extend the drying time.

Color washes gain depth and interest when closely related colors are layered together. Terra-cotta shades are especially warm and rich, while blues appear deep and mysterious, as if you were peering into a pool of water. The subtle variations that appear from color washing can help camouflage the minor imperfections on your wall such as cracks or an uneven plaster wall surface.

SPONGING

Sponging is easy and practically foolproof, making it especially attractive to beginners. Like rags, sponges can be used to apply glaze or diluted paint to a wall, to texture a layer of glaze that has already been applied, and to blot up glaze from the surface. There are two basic ways to maneuver a sponge. One way is to dab it up and down across the surface, so that the holes and impressions in the sponge create a negative imprint on the wall. This technique is most effective with a natural sea sponge because of the odd sizes and quirky shapes of its holes. As with a rag, be sure to rotate the sponge in your hand as you dab to avoid repeated patterns. When applying color, be sure to keep moving the sponge around. Don't linger too long in any one area or you will lose the detail and totally obliterate the background color.

The other method of sponging is to wipe the edge of the sponge lightly across the surface in short random strokes that resemble brushwork. If you lift the sponge slightly as you complete each stroke, you can create a lovely feathered effect that is especially effective when second and third colors are added. A large utility sponge works best for this technique.

If you are sponging off and the sponge becomes too paint-logged to continue, wring it out before proceeding. For smoother manipulation of glazes, moisten the sponge first. Water-based paints are preferred for sponging, but oil-based paints are workable, too. If you are concerned about water-based paints evaporating too quickly, sponge the wall with clear water before applying the glaze.

DRAGGING

Dragging produces the most pronounced texture and pattern of the four techniques discussed here. The glaze is always applied to the wall first, and then a comb is pulled or dragged through it in a straight line or with an undulating motion to create a pattern. You

can buy special painting combs with long teeth at art supply stores, or you can cut your own versions from coffee can lids or other stiff, smooth plastic. Brushes with stiff or short bristles are also suitable for dragging and can be used to produce wood-grain effects.

Dragging requires patience and precision. You must drag the comb or brush in a smooth continuous motion without any jerky stops or starts to mar the pattern. When you start a new "drag," you must move the comb directly alongside the previous drag to equalize the spacing and camouflage the join. Even movement and seamless joins are difficult to achieve on long ceiling-to-floor stretches that require climbing up and down on a stepladder. You may prefer to limit your first dragging effort to a more easily accessible area, such as the dado beneath a chair rail. Another option is to drag in short intersecting spurts, for crosshatching or basket-weave patterns that resemble coarsely woven fabric.

CLEANING UP

Painting a room is a big job, and the end-of-the-day cleanup can seem monumental if you don't approach it systematically. Water- and oil-based paints have different cleaning requirements, but each method will benefit by the use of a paintbrush spinner. This ingenious gadget, sold at paint and hardware stores, works like a child's hand-pumped spinning top to rotate a freshly cleaned wet brush or roller at a very high speed until it is almost dry. (Be sure to point the spinner down inside a deep bucket when you spin to contain the spray.)

To clean water-based paints, act promptly before the paint has a chance to harden. Rinse messy brushes and rollers under cool running water until all traces of paint are gone. Liquid dishwashing detergent can help loosen the paint and make it glide off more readily. Spin to remove the excess moisture, reshape the brush bristles as necessary, and lay the damp brushes or rollers on a table or counter

edge to dry. If the paint or glaze is particularly heavy or gloppy, rinsing and spinning several times in succession may be necessary. Plastic buckets can be rinsed clean in cool water.

Oil-based paints require a two-step cleanup process. First, you must use a solvent, such as turpentine or paint thinner, to break up and dissolve the paint, and then you must use sudsy water to wash away the solvent. Work in a well-ventilated area, and wear latex gloves to protect your hands. To clean a brush, pour a small amount of solvent into a clean plastic paint bucket and recap the original container. Dip the brush bristles into the solvent (holding the bucket at an angle to pool the solvent), then press the bristles against the inside wall of the bucket to release the pigment.

To clean oil-based paint from a roller, pour solvent into a flat pan with sides and set the roller in it, turning the roller to moisten the entire surface. The solvent will absorb only so much pigment, so if the brush or roller

SALVAGE TIPS

is particularly saturated, you may need to repeat this step several times with clear solvent to remove all the residue. To speed the cleaning, spin between the dippings. Follow up with a sudsy wash and a final spin. Damp brushes and rollers can then be left to dry as described in the paragraph on water-based paint cleanup. Buckets and tools can be cleaned by wiping with a rag dipped in solvent, then washed with soapy water and dried.

For economical and environmental reasons, used solvent should be recycled rather than poured down the drain. Pour the solvent into a clean glass jar, screw the cover on tightly, and set the jar in an out-of-the-way place where it won't be disturbed. In a week or two, the pigment will settle to the bottom, leaving behind clear solvent that can be reused.

Before your fancy takes flight, here are a few earthly suggestions about finding, buying, and reusing salvage.

• **Finding it.** Architectural salvage is all over the place, but the more fixed up and refurbished it is, the more it will cost. The obvious places to start are salvage emporiums, warehouses, or yards—check the phone book for listings. Flea markets are good sources for smaller pieces, as are auctions. Construction tradespeople often save architectural remnants: if you know any contractors, tell them what you are looking for. This holds true for architects and antique dealers, too, though they are more inclined to be pricey. If you're adventurous, you can approach a demolition crew at work, but because such sites are dangerous, you may get the brush-off. If you're clear about what you want, though, and have a little cash handy, they may oblige you.

• **Buying it.** Everything is negotiable. If the price of a refurbished item is too high, ask if there are similar pieces "as is," for they should cost less.

• **Moving it.** If your prized find is heavy, give the seller ten or twenty bucks to haul it to your place; it's cheaper than a new automobile seat cover or back surgery. If you do carry the treasure home yourself, always bend your knees when you lift. Likewise, if you tie your weighty find to a roof rack, use rope or tiedown straps. Do not resort to "heavy" string, baling twine, or anything else not up to the job. Looking into the rearview mirror and seeing your new stained glass door scattered across three lanes of swerving cars is no fun.

• **Reusing it.** If you are putting old plumbing or electrical fixtures back into commission, have them checked out by a plumbing or electrical-parts supply house first—or by an appropriate tradesperson. Although safety is your main concern, such suppliers can also be wonderful sources for those tiny little screws and odd-size fittings that hold everything together. And if you are thinking of putting salvaged masonry in a place where it could fall and hurt someone—say, setting a stone capital into a brick wall—you should hire a mason to do it. Choosing the correct mortar and supporting the piece while the mortar dries are best handled by professionals.

With a few well-chosen pieces of salvage here and there, your house will be more interesting, more lively, and more creative—in short, more like you.

Designers

DESIGNERS

DESIGNERS

John Abrams
South Mountain Company
Martha's Vineyard, MA
(508) 645-2618

Stamberg Aferiat
Architecture
New York, NY
(212) 255-4173

Margot Alofsin
Los Angeles, CA
(310) 395-8008

Anderson/Swartz
New York, NY
(212) 741-3021

Ann Sacks Tile & Stone
Portland, OR
(503) 281-7751

Marc Appleton
Los Angeles, CA
(310) 399-9386

Artistic Bath
Paramus, NJ
(201) 670-6100

Louann Bauer
San Francisco, CA
(415) 621-7262

Christine Belfor, tile
designer
New York, NY
(212) 722-5410

Ward Bennett
New York, NY
(212) 580-1358

Michael Berman
Los Angeles, CA
(213) 655-9813

Nick Berman
Los Angeles, CA
(310) 476-6242
(310) 471-9637

Larry Bogdanow
Bogdanow and Associates,
Architects
New York, NY
(212) 966-0313

J.S. Brown Design
Pasadena, CA
(818) 304-9701

Anthony P. Browne, Inc.
Washington, D.C.
(202) 333-1903

Butlers of Far Hills
Far Hills, NJ
(908) 234-1764

Peter Carlson
Deamer & Phillips,
Architects
New York, NY
(212) 925-4564

Carlson Chase Associates
Los Angeles, CA
(213) 969-8423

Celeste Cooper Group
Boston, MA
(617) 266-2288

Steven Chase
Palm Springs, CA
(619) 324-4602

Color Tile
Fort Worth, TX
(817) 870-9400

Francois deMenil, Architect, P.C.
New York, NY
(212) 779-3400

Gustavson Dundes
New York, NY
(212) 251-0212

Steven Ehrlich
Santa Monica, CA
(310) 828-6700

Charlotte Forsythe
Mary Prentiss Inn
Cambridge, MA
(617) 661-2929

Madeline Gesser
Hewlett Harbor, NY
(516) 374-7821

Joseph Giovaninni
New York, NY
(212) 2997-0980

Lou Goodman
New York, NY
(212) 243-4236

Gail Green
NewYork, NY
(212) 980-1098

Grunig/Wertz Architects
New York, NY
(212) 736-0890

Mary Ann Hall
Hall Design Associates
Denver, CO
(303) 839-9395

Jarett Hedborg
Los Angeles, CA
(310) 271-1437

Margaret Helfan
Architects
New York, NY
(212) 779-7260

David Hering
New York, NY
(212) 245-5371

Ronn Jaffe
Potomac, MD
(301) 365-3500

Lloyd Jafvert
Minneapolis, MN
(612) 897-5001

Debra Jones
Los Angeles, CA
(310) 476-1824

Cheryl and Jeffrey Katz
C & J Katz Studio, Inc.
Boston, MA
(617) 367-0537

Richard Kazarian
Richard Kazarian Antiques
Providence, RI
(401) 331-0079

Kennedy-Wilson International
Santa Monica, CA
(310) 314-8400

Neil Korpinen
Los Angeles, CA
(213) 661-9861

William Ku
Rochester Hills, MI
(313) 650-1300

Grant Larkin
West Stockbridge, MA
(413) 698-2599

Bently Larosa Salasky
New York, NY
(212) 255-7827

Vince Lattuca
Visconti & Company, Ltd.
New York, NY
(212) 758-2720

Shana Lev
New York, NY
(212) 496-8087

Michele Lewis
Lewis and Gould
New York, NY
(212) 807-6588

Jeffrey Lincoln
Locust Valley, NY
(516) 759-6100

Karen Linder
New York, NY
(212) 598-0559

The Little River Inn
Little River, CA
(707) 937-5942

David Livingston Interior Design
San Francisco, CA
(415) 392-2465

Janet Lohman Design
Los Angeles, CA
(310) 471-3955

Mark Mack
San Francisco, CA
(415) 777-5305

Adolf de Roy Mark,
Architect
Carefree, AZ
(602) 488-2216

Mayo-DeLucci Interiors
New York, NY
(212) 752-2762

Moore, Rubel, and Yudell
Mill Valley, CA
(213) 450-1400

Brian Murphy
Santa Monica, CA
(310) 459-0955

Nanticoke Associates
New York, NY
(212) 925-3611

Nobless Oblige
New York, NY
(212) 593-6100

Benjamin Nutter,
Architect
Topsfield, MA
(508) 887-9836

Barbara Ostrom
Associates
Mahwah, NJ
(201) 529-0444
New York, NY
(212) 465-1808

Tom O'Toole
New York, NY
(212) 348-0639

George Padilla
Pasadena, CA
(213) 254-0636

Bob Patino
Patino Limited
New York, NY
(212) 355-6581

Allie Chang Paul
Santa Monica, CA
(310) 459-1081

Florence Perchuk
New York, NY
(212) 421-1950

Tenold Peterson
Tenold Peterson Studios/Fine
  Glass Art
Junction City, OR
(503) 998-2750

Mark A. Polo
Polo, M.A. Inc.
Fort Lee, NJ
(201) 224-0322

Nancy Goslee Power
Los Angeles, CA
(310) 396-4765

Andrew Reczkowski
Chelsea, MA
(617) 884-4365

Gayle Reynolds, ASID
Lexington, MA
(617) 863-5169

Rhomboid Sax
Los Angeles, CA
(310) 550-0170

Charles Riley
New York, NY
(212) 473-4173
Los Angeles, CA
(213) 931-1134

Perry Dean Rogers
  and Partners,
  Architects
Boston, MA
(617) 423-0100

Bently Larosa Salasky
New York, NY
(212) 255-7827

Tom Sansone
New York, NY
(212) 966-3561

Schwartz/Silver Architects
Boston, MA
(617) 542-6650

Peter Shire
Los Angeles, CA
(213) 662-5385
(213) 662-8067

Shope, Reno, Wharton,
Architects
Greenwich, CT
(203) 869-7250

Debby Smith
Newburyport, MA
(508) 465-2435

Michael Smith
Los Angeles, CA
(310) 278-9046

Brenda Speight
Fredricksburg, TX

Bill Spink
Spink, Inc.
New York, NY
(212) 226-8022

Stephenson's Construction
Attleboro, MA
(508) 222-8191

Benn Theodore
Benn Theodore, Inc.
Boston, MA
(617) 227-1915

Truewest Designs
Clackamas, OR
(503) 658-8753

Van Hattum/Simmons
New York, NY
(212) 593-5744

Peter Wheeler
P.J. Wheeler Associates
Boston, MA
(617) 426-5921

David Wilson
  Design
South New Berlin, NY
(607) 334-3015

Robert Wine
Birmingham, MI
(810) 642-2317

Scott Wylie
Springfield, OR
(503) 741-8385

ARCHITECTURAL SALVAGE

Architectural Antiques Exchange
715 North Second Street
Marion, PA 19123
(610) 664-4559

Architectural Antiques, Ltd.
812 Canyon Road
Santa Fe, NM 87501
(505) 982-0042

Architectural Artifacts, Inc.
4325 North Ravenswood
Chicago, IL 60613
(312) 348-0622

The Brass Knob
2311 18th Street NW
Washington, DC 20009
(202) 332-3370

The Emporium
2515 Morse Street
Houston, TX 77019
(713) 528-3803

Gargoyles, Ltd.
512 South Third Street
Philadelphia, PA 19147
(215) 629-1700

Great Gatsby's Auction Gallery
5070 Peachtree Industrial
  Boulevard
Atlanta, GA 30341
(800) 428-7297

Queen City Architectural
Salvage
Box 16541
r, CO 80216
96-0925

One
outh Sangamon
go, IL 60608
733-0098

OGRAPHY CREDITS

r Aaron/Esto
graphics: p.46

illiam Abranowicz: p.217
; Design: Hall Design
Associates: pp.217 right, 247
right; Design: Judy Prouty: p.268
right

©Philip Beaurline: pp. 89, 123
right, 132 left

©James Brett: pp.31 left, 35 left

Courtesy of Color Tile, Fort
Worth, TX: pp.88, 106 right,
119 left, 133

©Grey Crawford: pp.14, 19,
27, 31 right, 34 right, 37 left,
47, 51, 55, 74, 75, 76, 79,
104, 120 left, 137, 157 right,
166 right, 168, 169 left, 171,
187, 190, 204 right, 237,
253

©Mark Darley/Esto Photographics: p.36

©Derrick & Love: p.30 right

©Daniel Eifert: Design:
Mayo-DeLucci Interiors, I.F.D.A.:
p. 122; as seen at MANSIONS
& MILLIONAIRES: 123 left;
Design: Bogdanow & Associates,
Architects: p.216

©Philip Ennis: pp.80-81, 93,
102 left, 106 left, 108, 109 left,
110, 117, 120 right, 125, 126,
134 right, 138, 139 right, 143,
223 right; Design: Visconti &
Company, Ltd.: p.265

©Feliciano: pp.65 left, 70, 77,
102 right

©Scott Frances/Esto
Photographics: pp.60, 71

©Michael Garland: pp.32 left
and right, 33, 58 left and right,
66 right, 69 left, 105 right, 136
right

©Tria Giovan: pp.6, 86, 105
left, 152, 153, 154 both, 158
right, 169 right, 174 left, 176,
177, 188, 197, 206, 224,
231, 242 right; Design: Michael
Foster: p.230

©Kari Haavisto: pp.193, 195
right

©Mick Hales: p.56, 181;
Design: Patino Limited: p. 233 left

©Rosmarie Hausherr: pp.213,
220, 221, 226 both, 229, 234
right, 235 right, 238 right, 244,
245 both, 249, 250, 251, 256
left, 264 right

©Nancy Hill: p.87; Photo
Courtesy of *House Beautiful's
Home Remodeling and Decorating
Magazine*: p.111 right; Design:
Madeline Gesser, courtesy of
*House Beautiful's Home
Remodeling and Decorating
Magazine*, The Hearst
Corporation: p.222; Design:
Nanticoke Associates: p.238 left;
Design: Stewart Witt: p. 223 left

©Image/Dennis Krukowski:
Design: Tom O'Toole: p.44 left;
Design: Harriette Levine Interiors:
p.44 right; Design: Anthony
Browne, Inc. Washington, D.C.:
p.49; Design: Brenda Speight,
Fredricksburg, TX: p.50; Design:
Jeffrey Lincoln Inc. Locust Valley,
NY.: p.67; Design: Sandra
Morgan, Inc.: p.146; Design:
Stone Age: pp.151, 195 left;
Design: Mary Dial: p.155;
Design: Ned Marshall Inc.:
pp.158 left, 170 left, 203 left;

Design: Robert Tartarini: p.164;
Architect: Donald Carruthers/inte-
rior design Suzanne O'Connell:
p.166 left; Design: Jeffrey Licoln
Inc.: p.172; Design: Michael
Lane: pp.174 right, 196 right;
Design: Tonin MacCallum
A.S.I.D., Inc.: p.179 top right;
Design: Brad Walker: p.179 bot-
tom left; Design: Marianne Von
Zastrow: p.196 left; Design:
Michael Tyson Murphy: pp.198,
203 right; Design: Lisa Rose:
p.199 right

©Jessie Walker Associates: p.228

©John Kane: p.94

©Balthazar Korab: pp.39, 43,
263 right, 264 left

©Tim Lee: pp.132 right, 246,
252

©Jennifer Levy: pp.99 bottom,
116

©David Livingston: pp.20, 28,
59 left, 68, 92 left, 100, 118,
119 right

©Mark Lohman: p.78

©Richard Mandelkorn: pp.109
right, 114, 128 right, 142, 183,
192 both; Design: Kennedy-
Wilson International: p. 209

©Michael Mundy: pp.90, 96 left, 97, 98, 99 top, 107, 115, 127, 128 left, 129; Design: Jed Johnson: p. 84

©Peter Paige: pp.66 left, 91 left, 103, 134 left; Design: Michele Lewis: p. 242 left; Design: Mark A. Polo: p. 255; Design: Charles Riley: p. 225

©Jack Parsons: pp.101, 135

©Robert Perron: Design: Conrad Malicoat: p.243; Design: Glass by David Wilson: p.214 left

©David Phelps: pp.82, 83, 85, 91 right, 92 right, 95, 96 right, 136 left, 215, 233 right, 235 left, 268 left; Design: Charles Chase Associates: p. 234 left; Design: Karen Linder: pp.240, 248; Design: Shope, Reno, Wharton, Architects: p.208

©Robert Reck: Design: Nathaniel Owings: p.239

©Paul Rochelau: pp.73, 212

©Eric Roth: pp.5, 22, 23, 40, 45 left & right, 52, 53, 57 left and right, 112, 214 right, 232, 254; Design: Charlotte Forsythe: p. 247 left; Design: C+J Katz Studio, Inc.: p.259; Design:

Richard Kazarian Antiques: p.267 top; Design: Stephenson's Construction: p.241; Design: P.J. Wheeler Associates: p.236

©Bill Rothschild: pp.139 left, 160, 200 left

©Richard Sexton: p.61

©Tim Street-Porter: pp.16, 26, 29, 34 left, 37 right, 38, 41, 48 left, 54, 65 right, 69 right, 72, 121, 124 both; Design: Jarett Hedborg: p.113; Design: Greene and Greene: p.111 left; Design: Mark Mack: p.130; Artist: Peter Shire: pp.131; 144, 156, 157 left, 159, 161 both, 162, 163, 165, 167, 170 right, 173, 175, 178, 180, 182, 184, 185, 186, 189, 191, 194, 199 left, 200 right, 202, 204 left, 205, 267 bottom; Design: Tom Callaway: p.262; Design: Tony Duquette: p.227; Design: Greene & Greene: p. 218, 219; Design: Jay Griffith: p. 269; Design: Holdeln & Dupuy: p. 260 right; Design: Landenberger & Waterman: pp. 211, 258; Design: Charles Moore: p.261; Design: Brian Murphy: pp.256 right, 257, 260 left; Design: Brian Murphy & Gale McCall: 266; Design: Charles Riley: p. 263 left

Courtesy of Truewest Designs: pp.62 left & right, 63

©Brian Vanden Brink: pp.8, 9, 11, 12, 147, 148, 149

©Paul Warchol: pp.30 left, 35 right, 48 right, 59 right, 64

INDEX